Jonathan Plass
Portfolio
Volume 01

Jonathan Plass
www.jonathanplass.com

ISBN-10 | 0-692-84775-8
ISBN-13 | 978-0-692-84775-6

Volume 01
Playfully for

Brian Shepherd

Edmond Plass, Barbara Schweizer, Ben Farrell, Shakiem Smith, Rob Hewitt, Conrad Haber, Byron Davis, Debra Hoffman, Michael Koehler, Susan Lowry, Meg Goldner Rabinowitz, Michael Williamson, Sarah Zwerling, Drew Paul Bell, Darin Jellison, Thomas Kirk, Sam Olshin, Aaron White, Chi-Fan Wong, and the Germantown Friends School Class of 2017

PREFACE

i

WHY I DESIGN

THE FIFTH AVENUE
APPLE STORE

My interest in design, and more specifically architecture, began a few days after my eleventh birthday.

I had received the third generation iPod Touch, which was advertised to be "The Funnest iPod Ever." However, my iPod was no fun at all. It was broken in the box when I opened it and was no better than a beautifully designed curved brick made of some of the best aluminum my virgin hands had ever touched. This mishap resulted in a long journey to the Apple store on 5th Avenue in New York. For my eleven-year-old self, this meant three bumpy, crowded, and loud subway rides from our house to get there. The ride there was horrific; all I thought about were the hours I had lost with my beautiful curved brick of aluminum. These hours did not seem to faze my mother as she read on the way there. Once out of the subway and at the Apple store, both of our jaws dropped, my eyes lit up, and my mother let out a horrendous groan. For those who don't know, the 5th Avenue Apple store is a glass cube with a glowing Apple logo that leads down to an underground store of sleek metal slabs. For my mother, the 5th Avenue Apple store was just an absurd line she had to queue up in to fix something she had already spent too much money buying me in the first place.

In line, I could barely stand still. The Apple store was like a wonderland for designers. It had small curved bricks of aluminum that played music, slightly larger curved bricks of aluminum that made phone calls, and large bricks of aluminum that unfolded to reveal a keyboard and a track pad. In addition, these bricks were positioned with all the negative space that even the most conceptual designer could ever wish for. The perfectly proportioned light wood tables floated underground in a sea of neutral grey concrete and stainless steel, impaled in the middle by a spiral glass staircase and elevator. This building was all too much for me, and two hours in line seemed like seconds. My eyes wandered around the space, stopping at every little detail I could detect, and then back over them again. This building single-handedly forced me to fantasize over the built environment, and this was the kindling of my journey to become a designer.

My pursuit started at age twelve when I told myself I would become an architect. From this moment, which seems like the start of it all, four years went by with no serious engagement. I was a "weekend warrior," so to speak, of architecture. I could build all of the Lego architecture sets from Frank Lloyd Wright's "Falling Water" to Frank Lloyd Wright's "Imperial Hotel." I could tell you that AutoCAD was the be-all and end-all of computer-aided drafting programs. Most importantly, I could predict the prices of mansions and apartments on House Hunters and more impressively House Hunters International. This phase lasted about four years and ended with my introduction to Google SketchUp.

Google SketchUp is a 3D computer modeling software that is free to use. I started with no knowledge, clicking almost blindly, just trying to make a cube. Eventually, cube after cube turned into a cube with a doorway, a cube with a doorway and windows, and my first design. A year later I attended Pratt's PreCollege Architecture program, which drew me even deeper into the field. The professors and the program encapsulated everything I thought and hoped architecture would be, all in one simple project. "Create a gallery or a library that integrates into campus, derived from an image of a brick zoomed in eight hundred times."

After this experience, I was in love with architecture and returned home as a slightly more sophisticated weekend warrior. I could build physical models, I could fumble my way around AutoCAD, and I watched every architecture lecture YouTube had to offer on the topic. I dived deeper into the field of architecture, landing my first internship at Bohlin Cywinski Jackson, ironically the firm that designed the 5th Avenue Apple store. This phase brings me up to the present and contains the entire basis for my pursuit of becoming an architect.

I design because I believe there is immense potential for architecture to improve the lived environment, promote positive human interaction, and because I cannot help but stare at one of those curved bricks of aluminum that Apple sells.

NISSHŌKI & KIMIGAYO

FLAGS, ANTHEMS, AND THEIR SOCIAL POWER

I was born April 23rd, 1999, the same year a few months from when the beautiful white rectangle and red circle were officially adopted by Japan. For me, this flag represents an inspiring culture, a great design, and an amazing country I long to visit. However, the same Japanese flag I love is filled with debate. The same Japanese flag that was made official the year I was born, was the same flag that led to a suicide the year I was born. To truly understand the Japanese flag, one must look back at the history of Japan and the events surrounding the design of the flag itself.

The Convention of Kanagawa on March 31, 1854, marked the end of Japan's 220 year seclusion. The Convention of Kanagawa was a treaty between the United States of America and what was Tokugawa Shogunate, now the Japanese government, that opened Japanese ports to American ships. This treaty, which the thirteenth U.S. president, Millard Fillmore, pushed for by using gunboat diplomacy, was driven by increased American trade with China, American whalers near Japanese waters, and British and French monopolization of coal in Asia. Japan's entrance into more open trade policies led to the need to define itself globally and the creation of the country's flags.

One of Japan's early flags, which defined the Tokugawa Shogunate rule, was a white rectangle with a centered, horizontal, black stripe. Next came the imperial flag of the Meiji period. This imperial flag had a red rectangle with a centered 16-petal golden chrysanthemum. This design was used nationally until 1870 and is currently used for the imperial flag. The first national flag of Japan was the white background and red circle you are used to seeing today, but the flag was 7 x 10 in ratio, and the circle was shifted 1% left of center. This flag, although adopted socially by the Japanese people in 1870, was never officially declared the national flag.

Seventy-five years later, after Japan's defeat in World War II, there were rumblings of establishing this flag officially. In 1974, legal attempts were made, but failed after opposition from the Japan Teacher Union. The Japan Teacher Union believed that the unofficial flag as well as the national anthem had relations to Japanese militarism and therefore should not be used. These arguments escalated, and in 1996 the education ministry forced public schools to raise the flag and sing the Kimigayo anthem. Reaching the argument's climax at the end of the 1999 school year, Toshihiro Ishikawa committed suicide in protest of the flag and anthem; he was a high school principal in Hiroshima.

Following this suicide, the Act on National Flag and Anthem was passed. This officially defined the national flag and anthem. The act made official a modified version of the flag that perfectly centered the red circle and used a more vibrant red. The flag was stated to be a white rectangle proportioned 2 by 3, with a centered red circle three-fifths the hoist in diameter. The act also made official the national anthem, "Kimigayo."

The Japanese flag represents purity and power while also emphasizing the simplistic Japanese aesthetic. Interpreting the Japanese flag, the white background represents honesty and purity. The red circle represents the sun goddess Amaterasu. Amaterasu is an important figure in Japanese mythology, as she is said to be a direct relative of Japanese emperors.

Translating "Kimigayo," the national anthem, reveals sentiments of an emperor's power, which shines light on prior Japanese militarism. "Kimigayo" translates directly to

> "May your reign
> Continue for a thousand,
> Eight thousand generations,
> Until the pebbles
> Grow into boulders
> Lush with moss."

"Kimigayo" also poetically translates to:

> "Thousands of years of happy reign be thine;
> Rule on, my lord, until what are pebbles now
> By ages united to mighty rocks shall grow
> Whose venerable sides the moss doth line."

Comparing the two, they both perpetuate the previous empire and militaristic history of Japan, but differ in the light they use to portray the empire. Both translations promote the idea that the emperor should reign for thousands of years. This idea refers back to the old empires, 1868 to 1947, which existed under the slogan "Fukoku Kyōhei," or "Enrich the Country, Strengthen the Armed Forces." Comparing the two, the plain translation is neutral in tone, but the poetic version offers praise to the empire by describing the reign as "happy." Together, the translations give the idea that the national anthem perpetuates Japanese militarism.

Although many see the white rectangle and centered red circle as a superb example of flag design that represents Japan, I see it and its historical controversy. I see flags as major statements about each country as well as pieces of art. Flags are designed to embody a country visually. The fifty stars on the American flag, the maple leaf of Canada, the Swiss cross—these flags and their details all portray and embed a snippet of each country's culture and history. Flag design is so much more than just design; it is history, sociology, anthropology. These areas of study give the flags their weight and the designs give them their power. Some flags are beautiful pieces of design genius. Japan, Canada, Switzerland, and Albania all have beautifully simplistic designs that capitalize on some historical detail or cultural element of the country. This beauty allows and encourages citizens to rally behind their nation or gain a glimpse into another country. These small glimpses of history and culture that flags provide, as well as the social rallying power they have, makes me believe that flag design is one of the most important and politically involved art forms.

BODY ii

ARCHITECTURE

What should our designs try to achieve? We must take a critical look at the brief, make it more comprehensive. We must look beyond the narrow object and ask ourselves: What will be the ecological consequences?

Sir Ove Arup

PRATT LIBRARY ADDITION

The Pratt Library Addition was designed as my final project for the Pratt PreCollege Architecture program I attended in the summer of 2015. The assignment was to design a library for Pratt's Brooklyn Campus in New York. Integrated directly onto an existing campus building, my library addition is a convenient and striking addition to the compact Brooklyn campus.

Pratt's PreCollege Architecture program is a one month intensive summer program on Pratt's Brooklyn campus in New York. The program includes architecture, foundation, art history and portfolio development.

For more details visit
www.pratt.edu

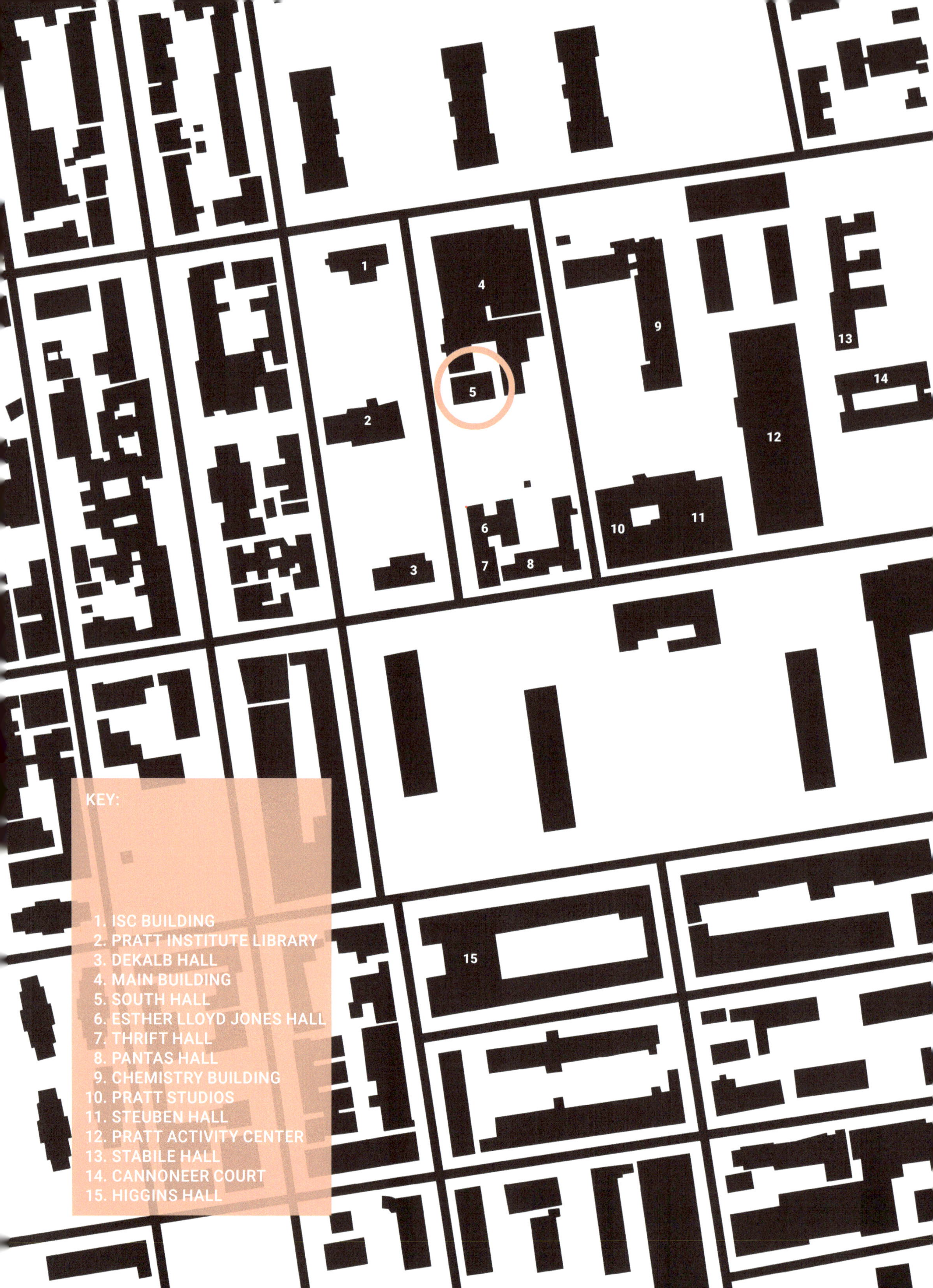
1
2
3
4
5
6
7
8
9
10
11
12
13
14
15
KEY:
1. ISC BUILDING
2. PRATT INSTITUTE LIBRARY
3. DEKALB HALL
4. MAIN BUILDING
5. SOUTH HALL
6. ESTHER LLOYD JONES HALL
7. THRIFT HALL
8. PANTAS HALL
9. CHEMISTRY BUILDING
10. PRATT STUDIOS
11. STEUBEN HALL
12. PRATT ACTIVITY CENTER
13. STABILE HALL
14. CANNONEER COURT
15. HIGGINS HALL

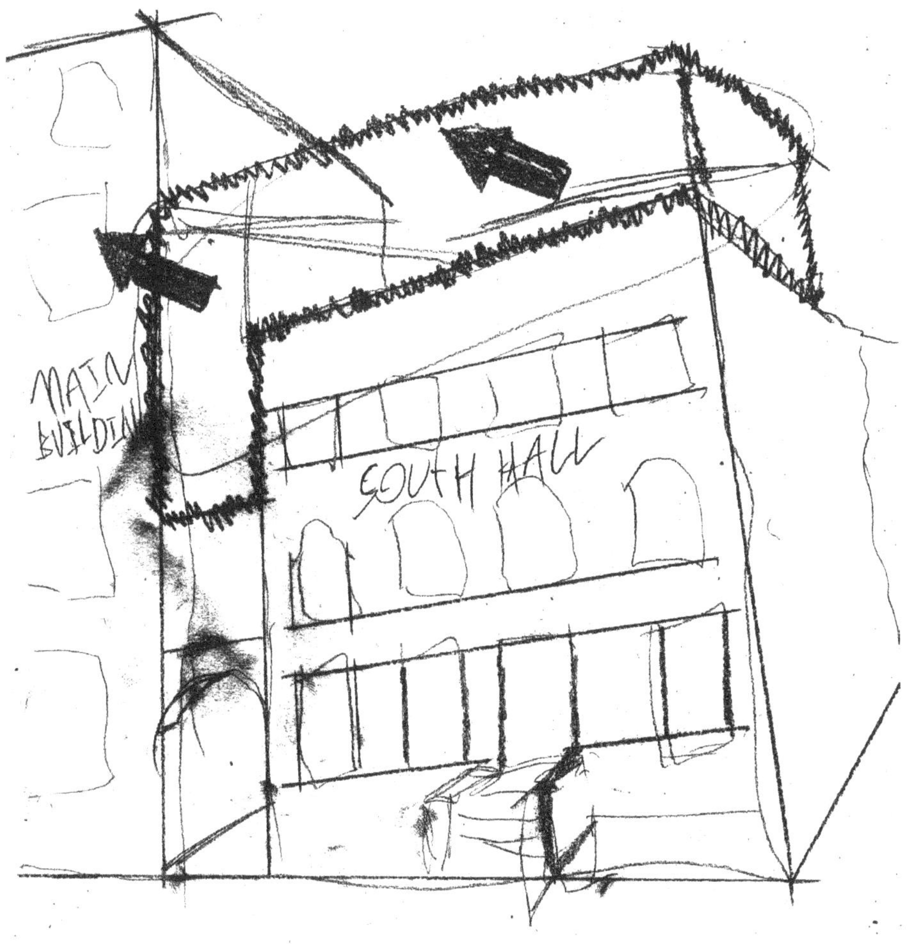

The first step in the design process of this library was figuring out where to locate the structure. Pratt's Brooklyn campus is fairly compact, while still maintaining lots of green areas. Pratt's campus is public and contains sculptures throughout, which I did not want to interrupt with the addition of a library. This predicament led to the initial design of the library to be attached to the Main Building and resting on top of the South Hall. Programming the space, responses to the site were created to answer the needs of the building. Further into the programming phase, space was tight, causing the building to be extruded over the front of the South Hall.

First, a photograph of bricks was taken. Then the image was zoomed in eight hundred times and put into grayscale. Next, the general shapes were traced using horizontal and vertical lines to map the major forms. From here, a study model was made.

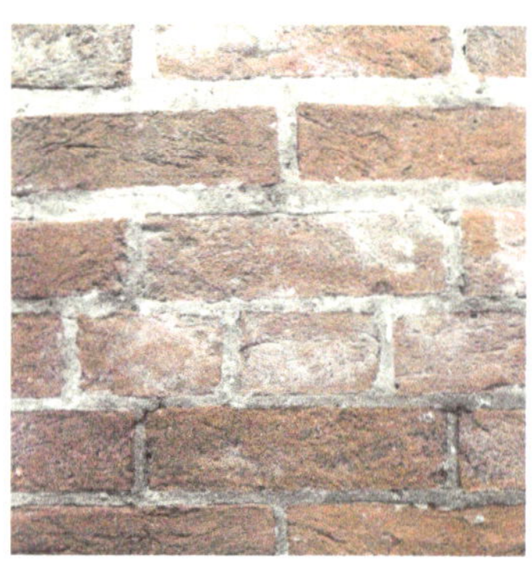

I

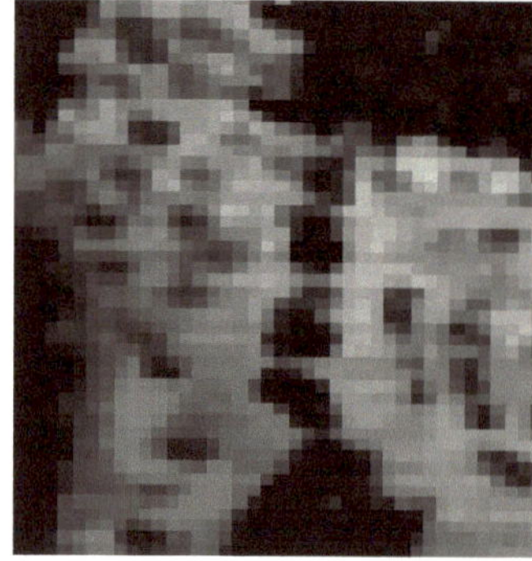

II

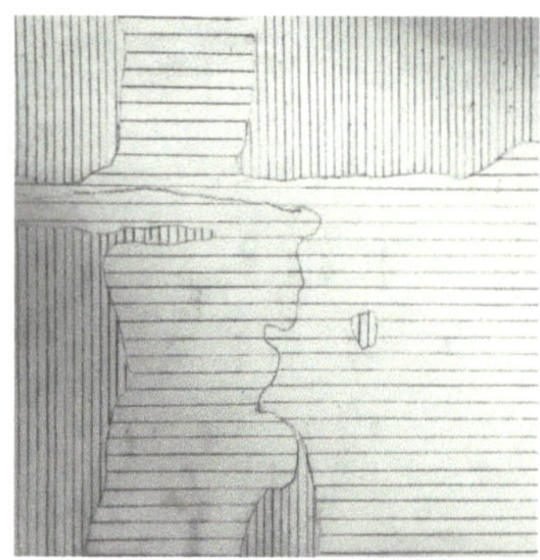

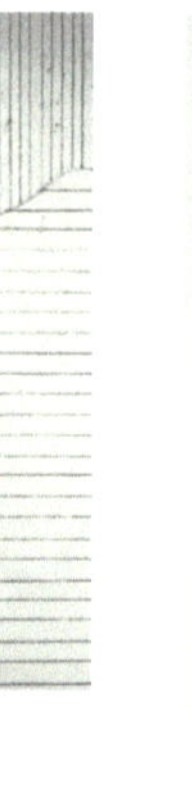

III

Looking towards the site to begin to flesh out the design. The Pratt Main Building and the area that surrounded it had limited ground space for new construction. This restraint led the building to rest on top of the lower section of the main building.

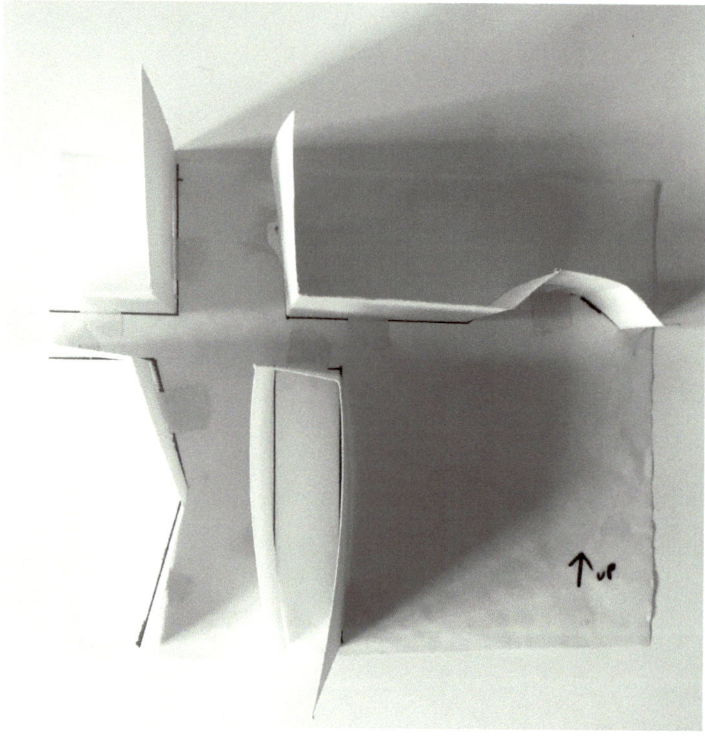

IV

I initial brick photograph

II brick photograph at 800× converted to black and white

III trace of bricks at 800× with varying horizontal and vertical lines

IV study model extruding the main lines from the trace sketch

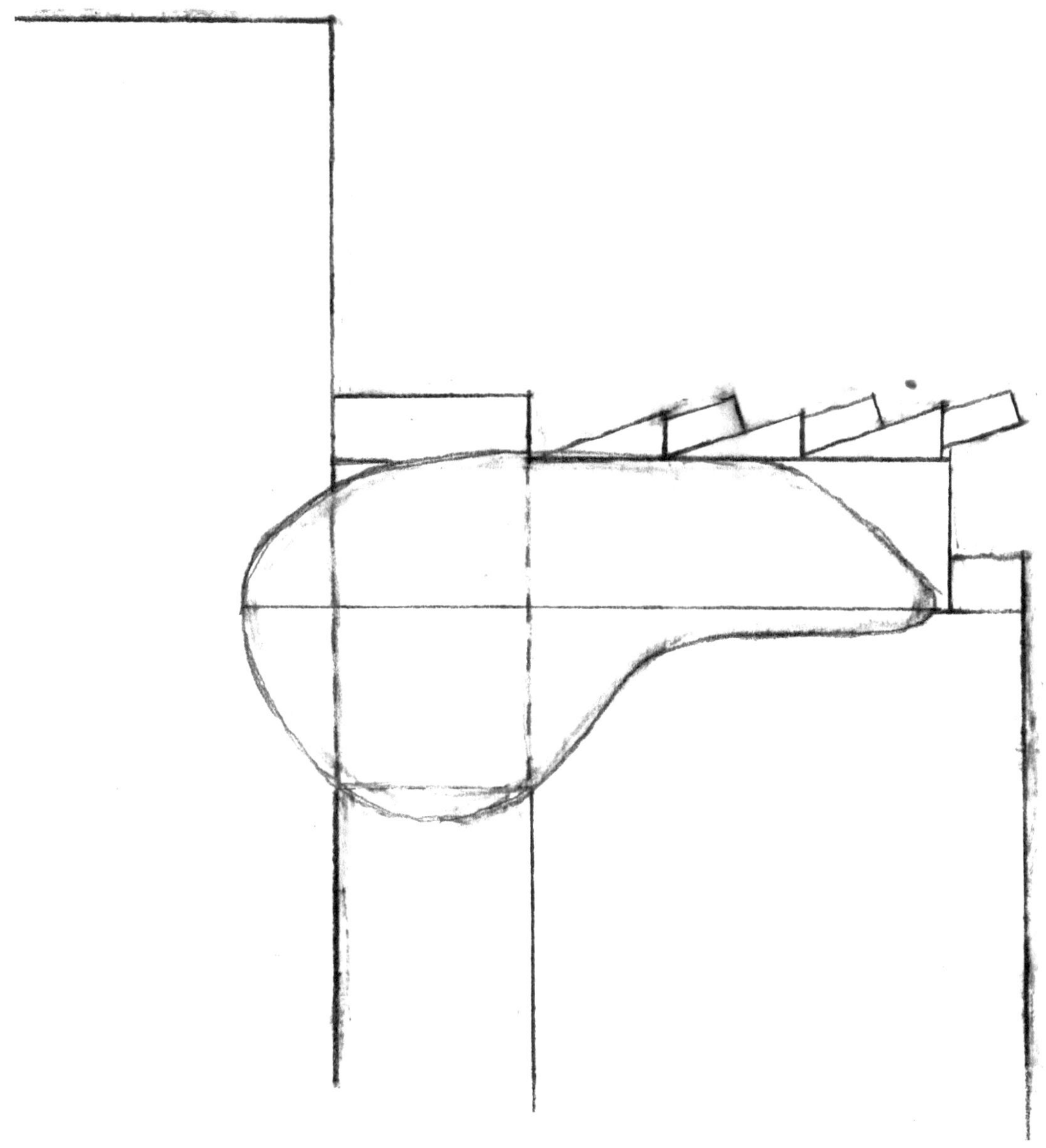

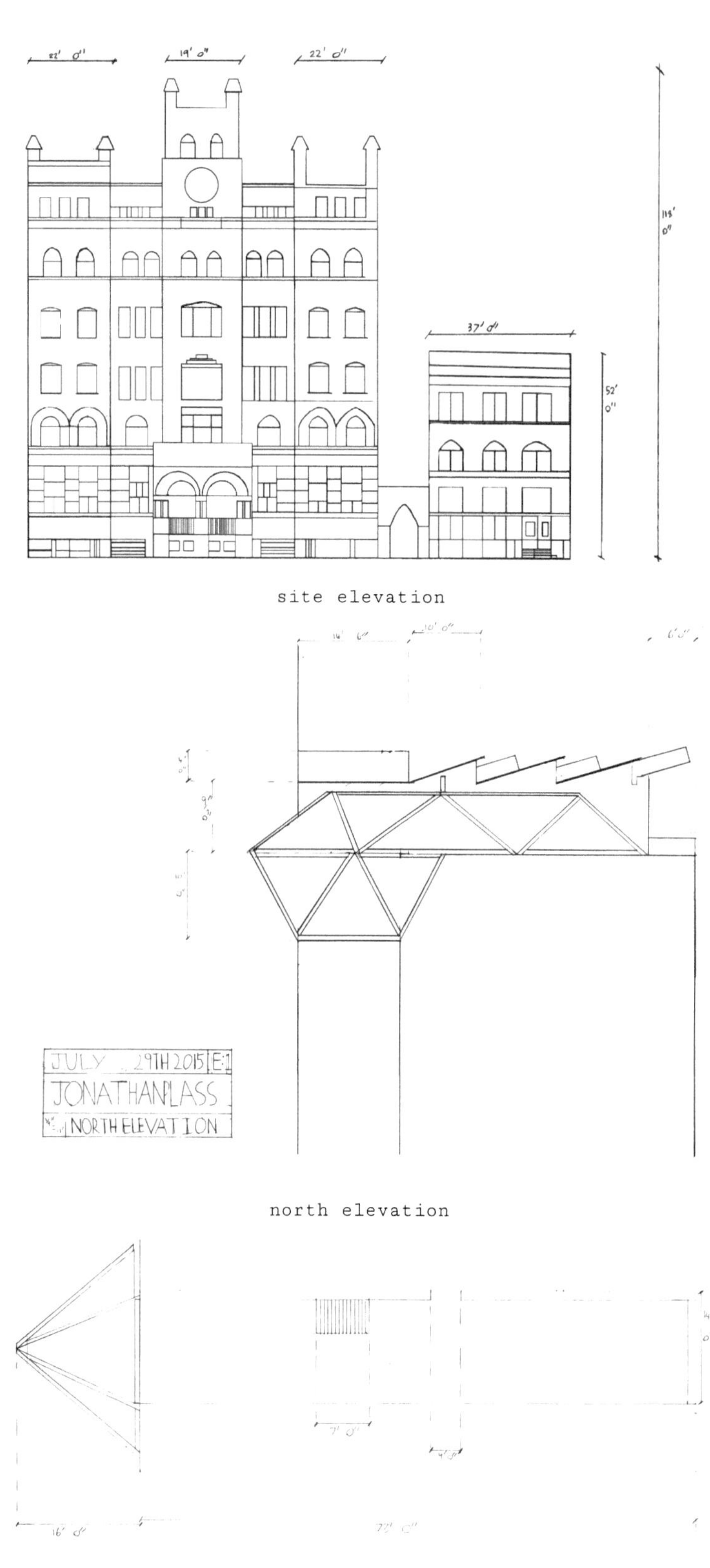

site elevation

north elevation

lower level plan

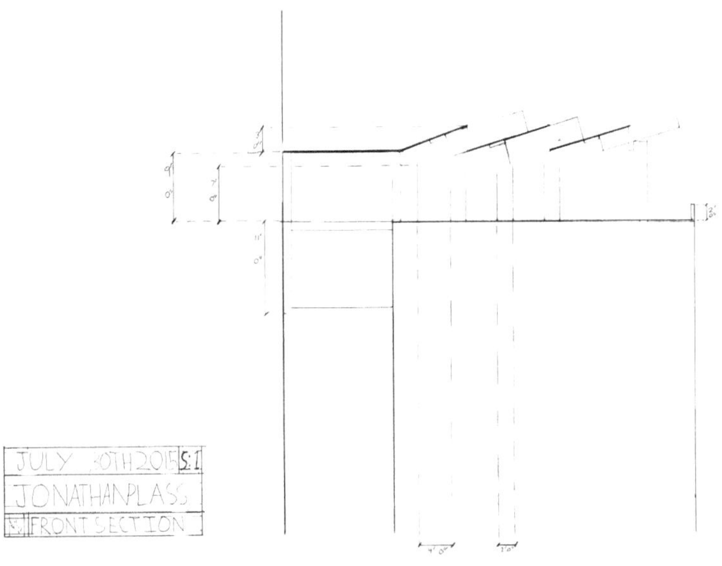

front section

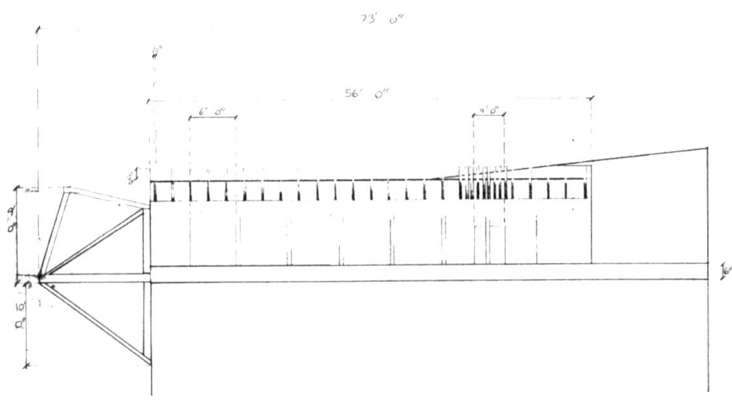

east elevation

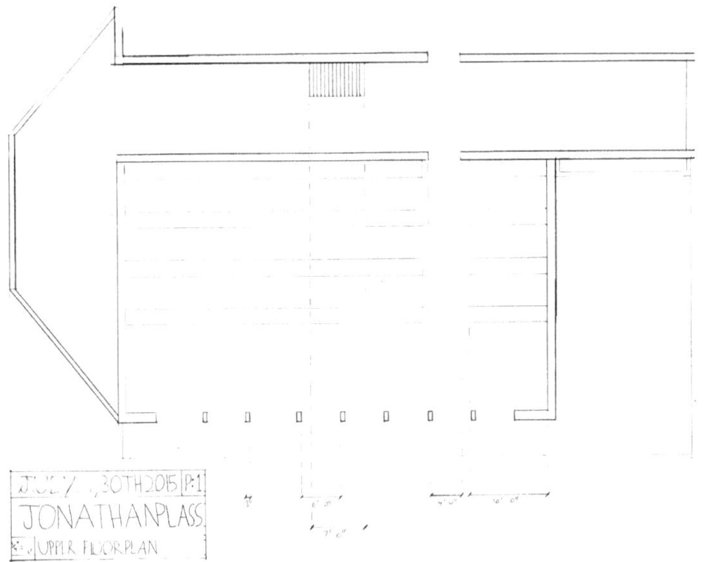

upper level plan

model scale:
1/4" to 1'
21.5" × 18" × 24"

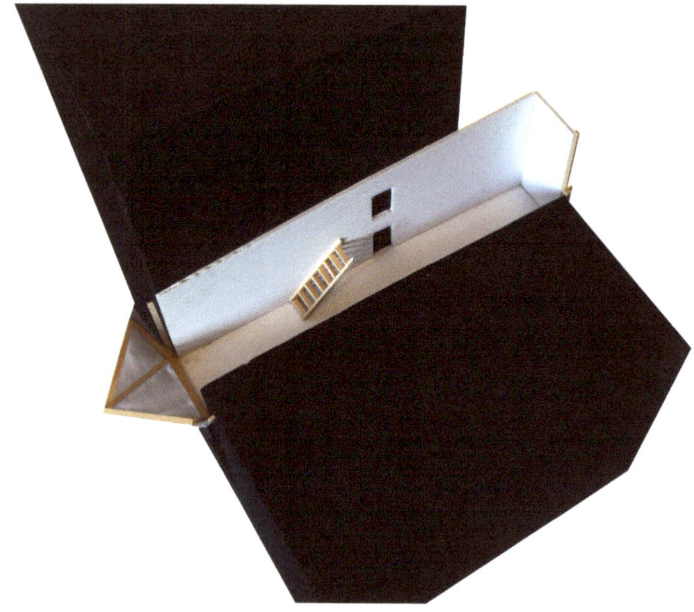

lower level

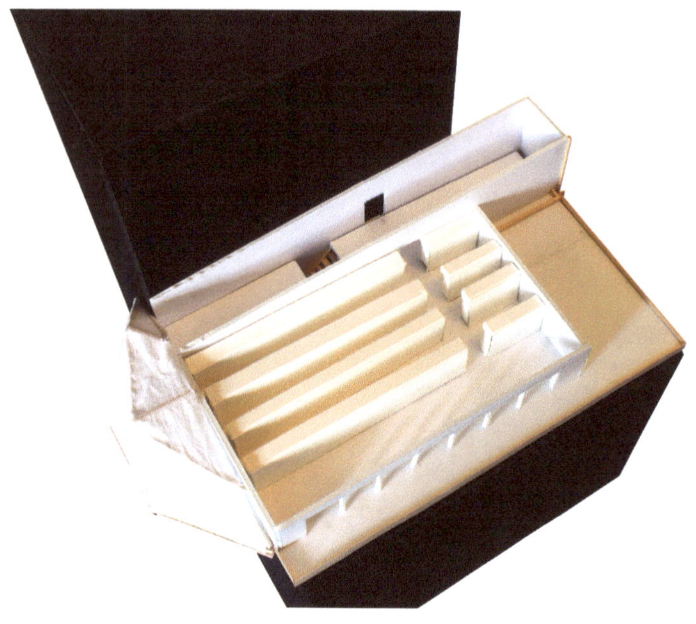

upper level

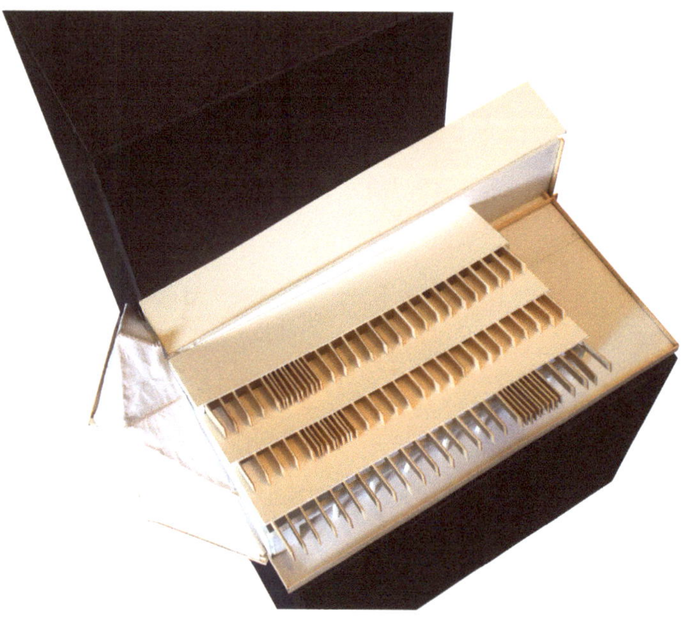

exterior

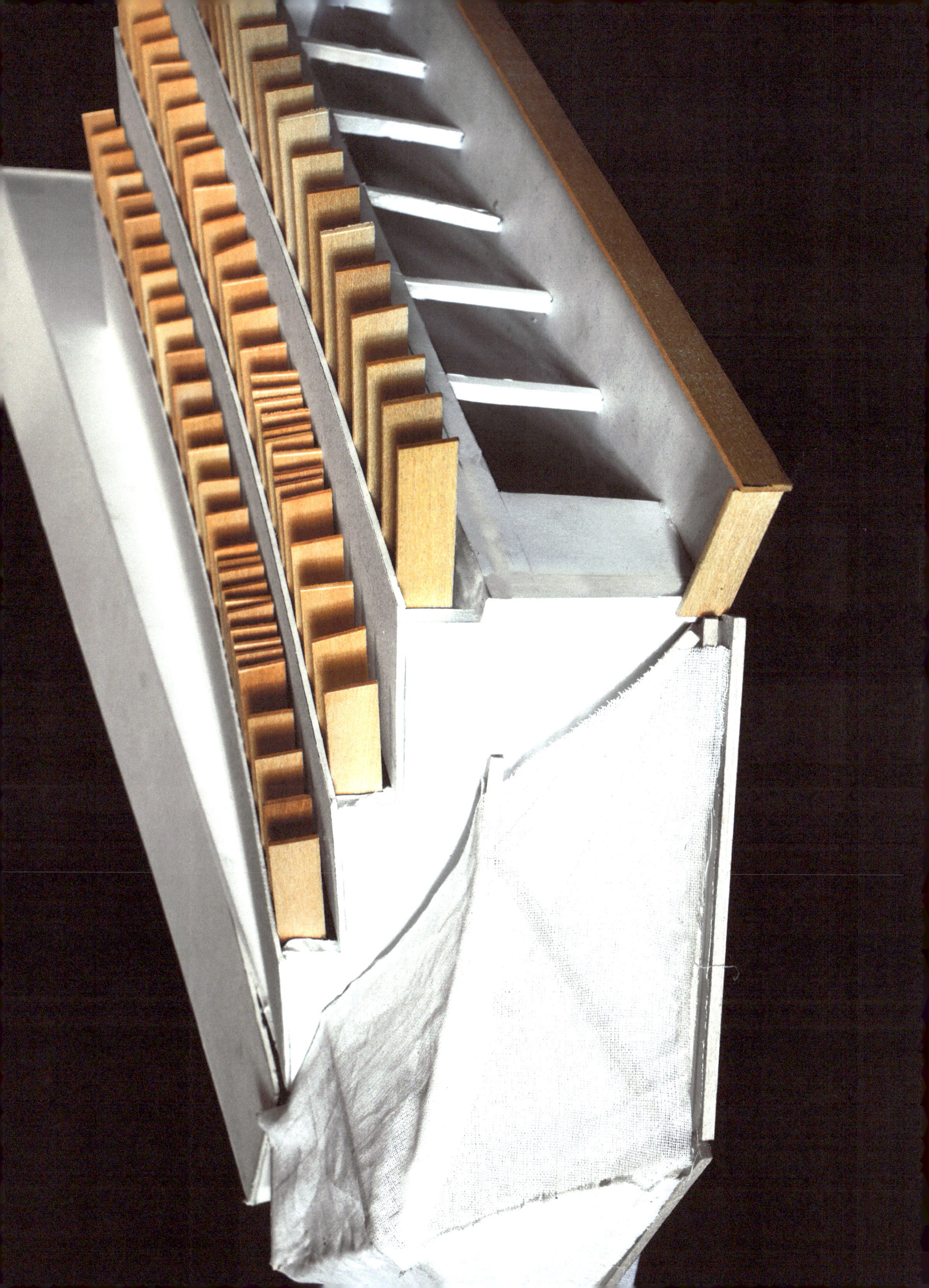

WITHOUT WALLS: GLOBAL ONLINE ACADEMY

“Without Walls” was a project completed for Global Online Academy Architecture course during the spring of 2016. The assignment was to create a one-room structure. For the project type I chose residential, as it allowed for a more personal design. The idea driving this project was to play with creating distinct spaces without using traditional floor-to-ceiling walls.

Global Online Academy is an online school created to give students from across the globe access to intellectually rigorous programs in effective and new ways. Global Online Academy Architecture covered elements of architectural design, materials and structure, architectural analysis, and 3D design.

For more details
www.globalonlineacademy.org

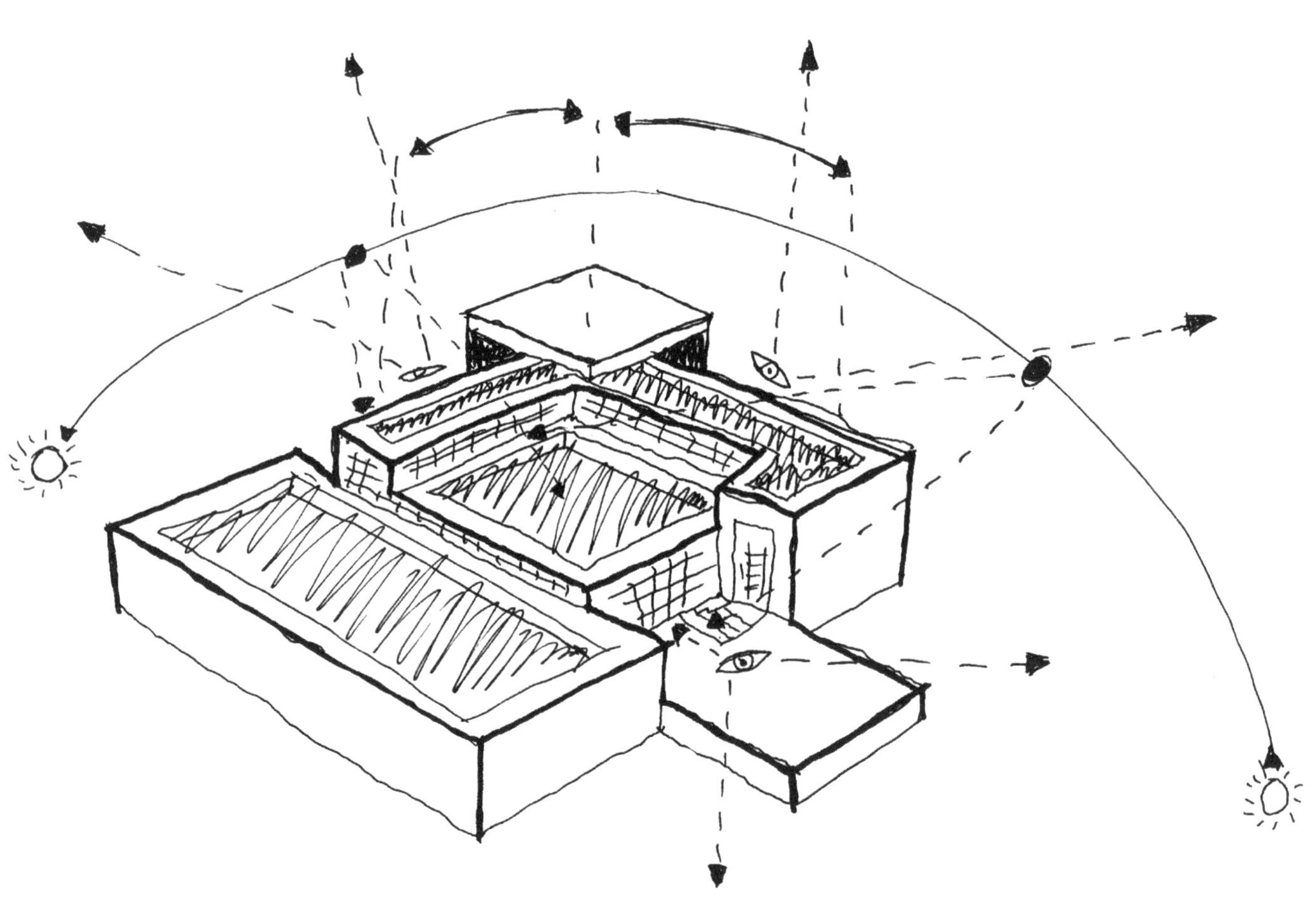

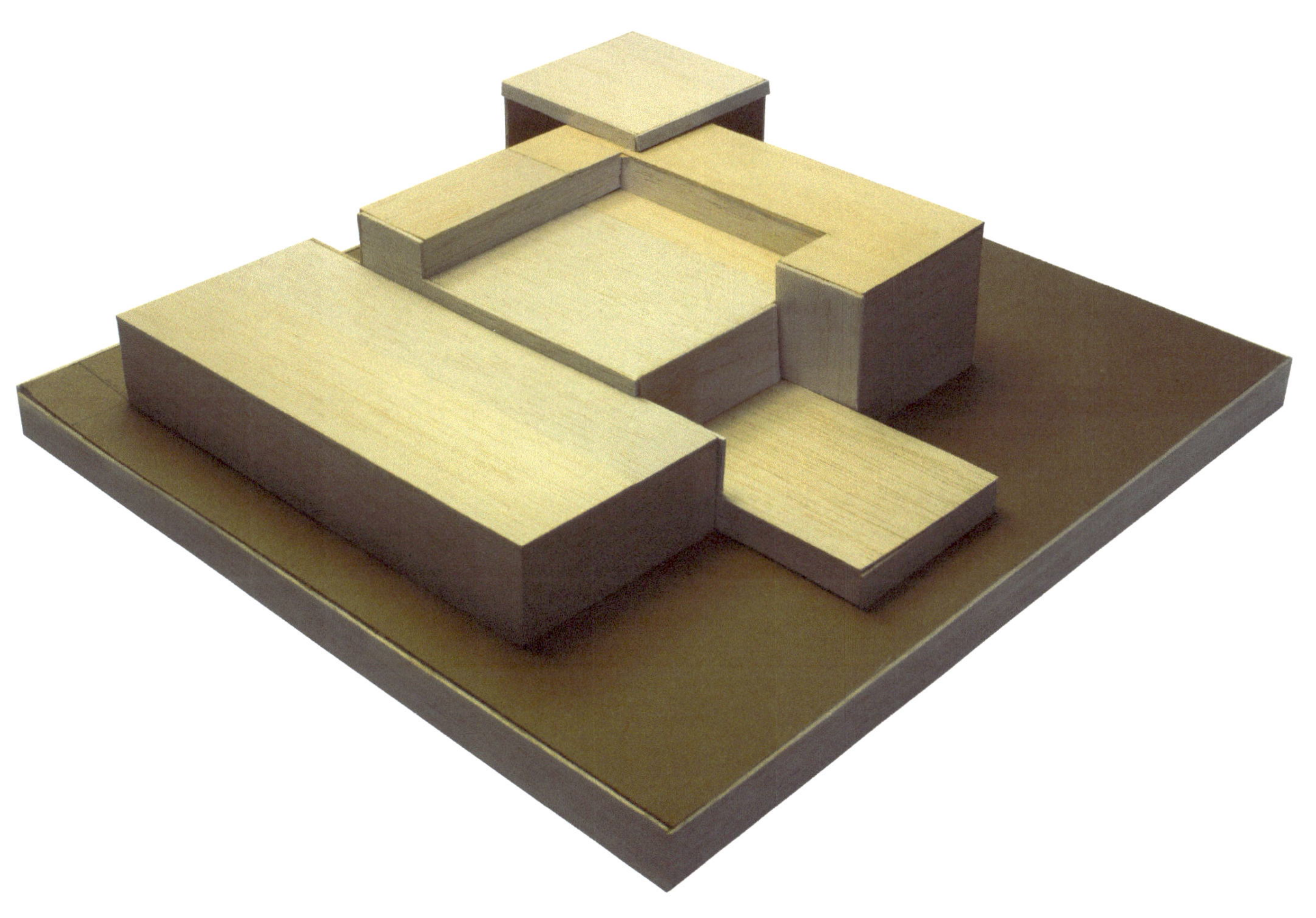

model scale:
1/4" to 1'
16" × 18" × 5"

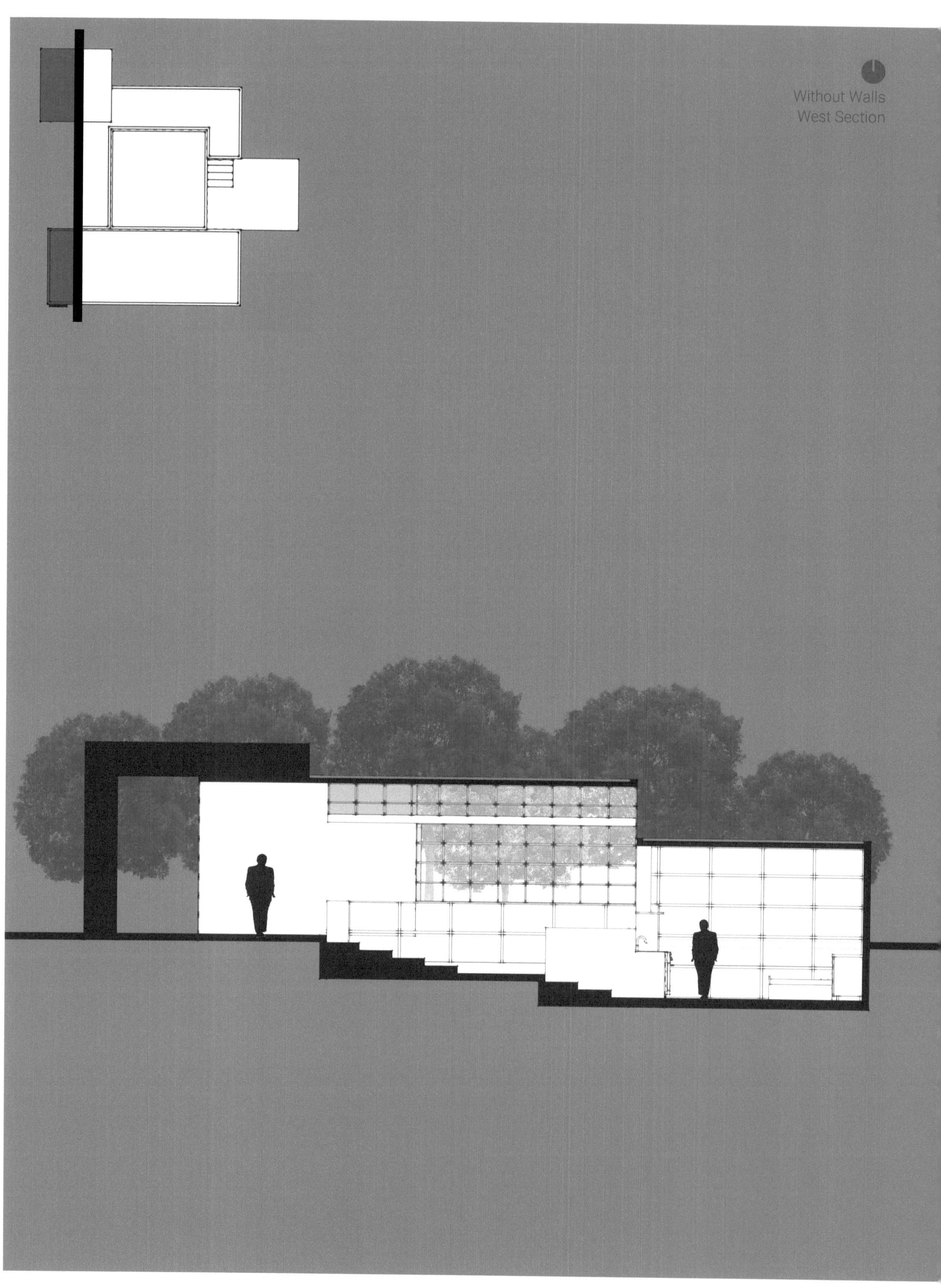
Without Walls
West Section

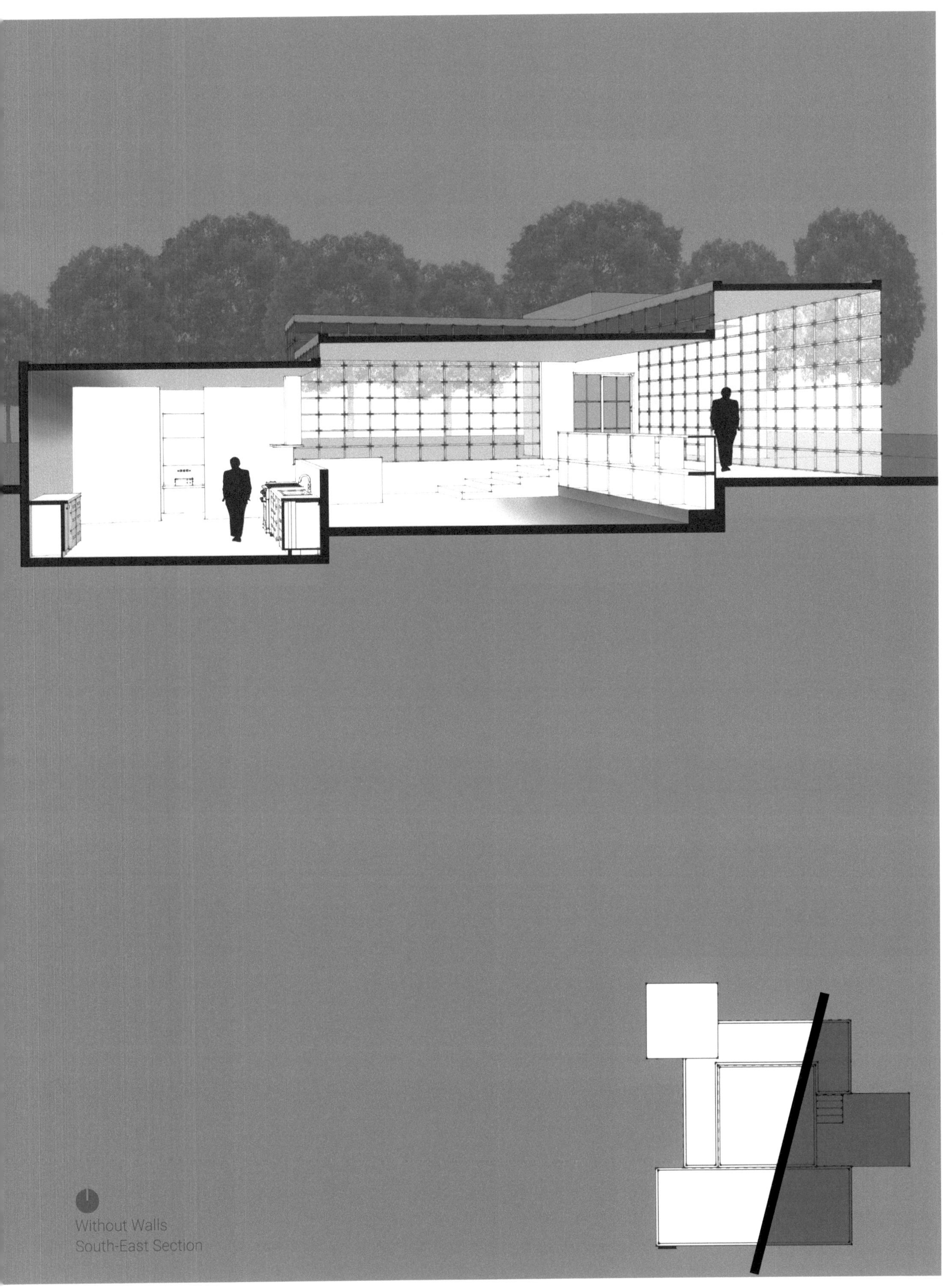
Without Walls
South-East Section

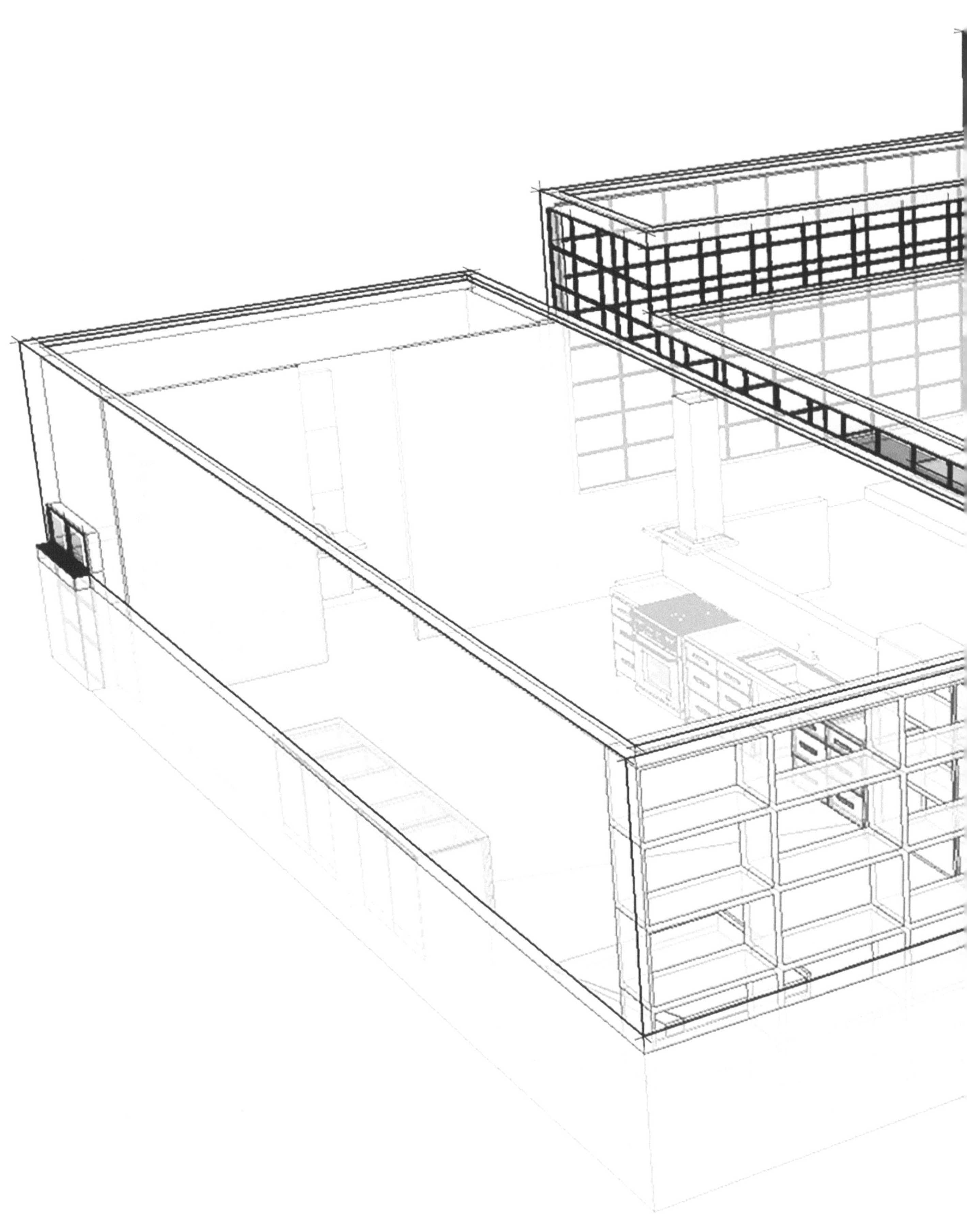

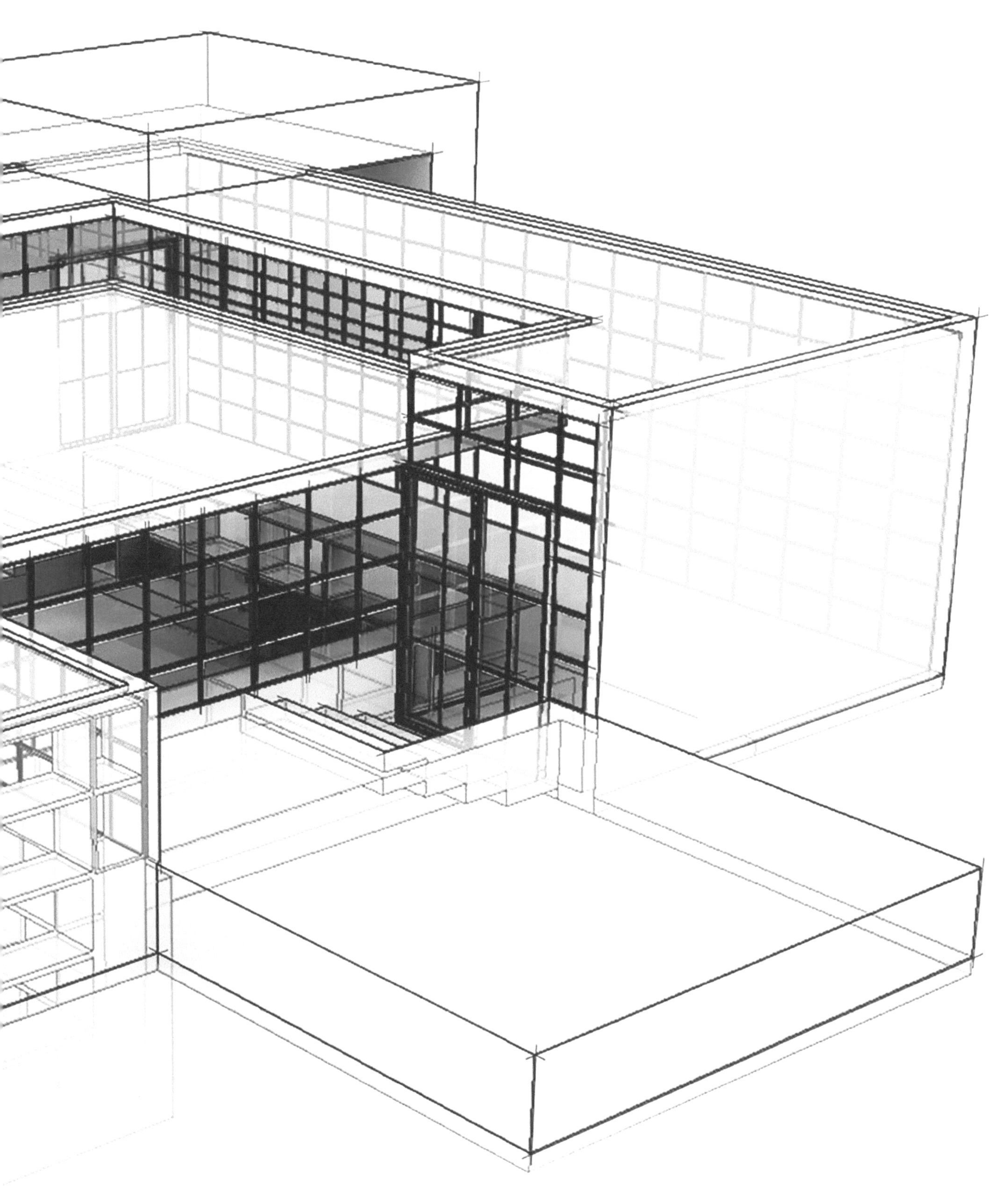

SCULPTURE

My goal is to strip things down so that you need just the right amount of words or shape to convey what you need to convey. I like editing.
I like it very tight.

Maya Lin

FERNS STUDY

"Ferns Study" was a research and process-oriented project from my directed independent study in architecture my junior year of high school. The project goal was to observe nature, break down its forms, and then create something new based upon that reduced form. This sculpture is one of many variants of forms based on nature that I created throughout the project.

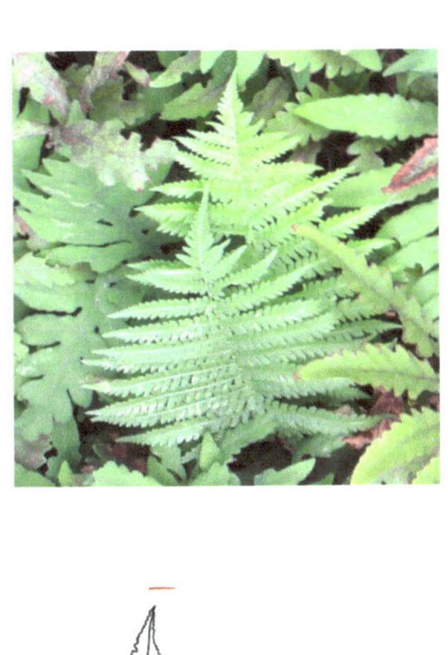

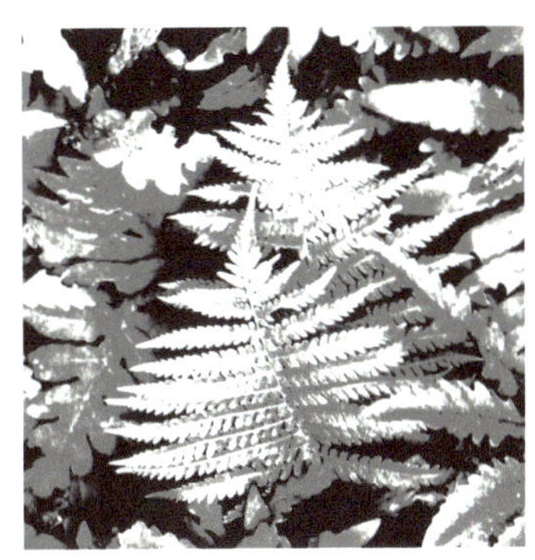

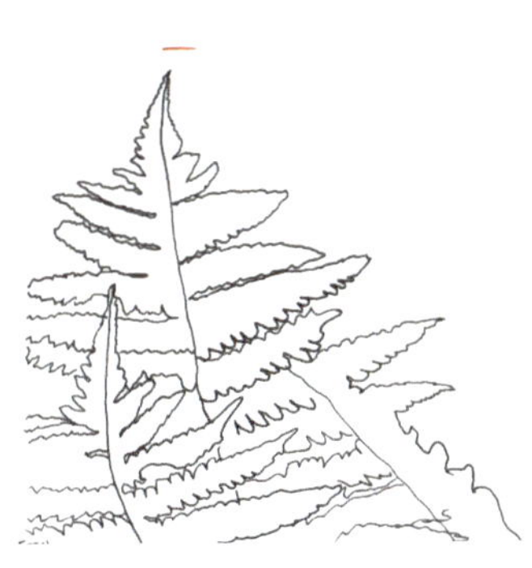

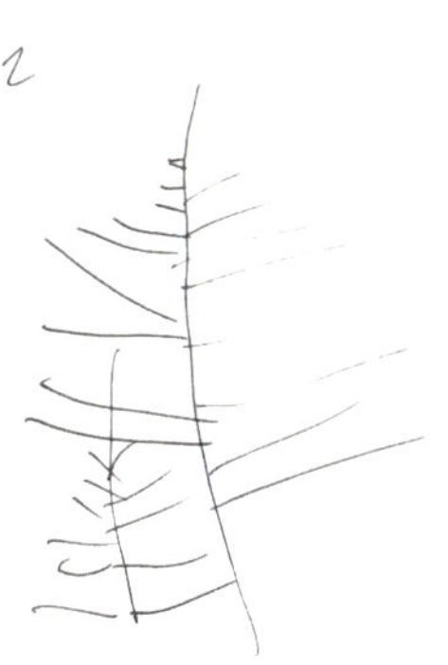

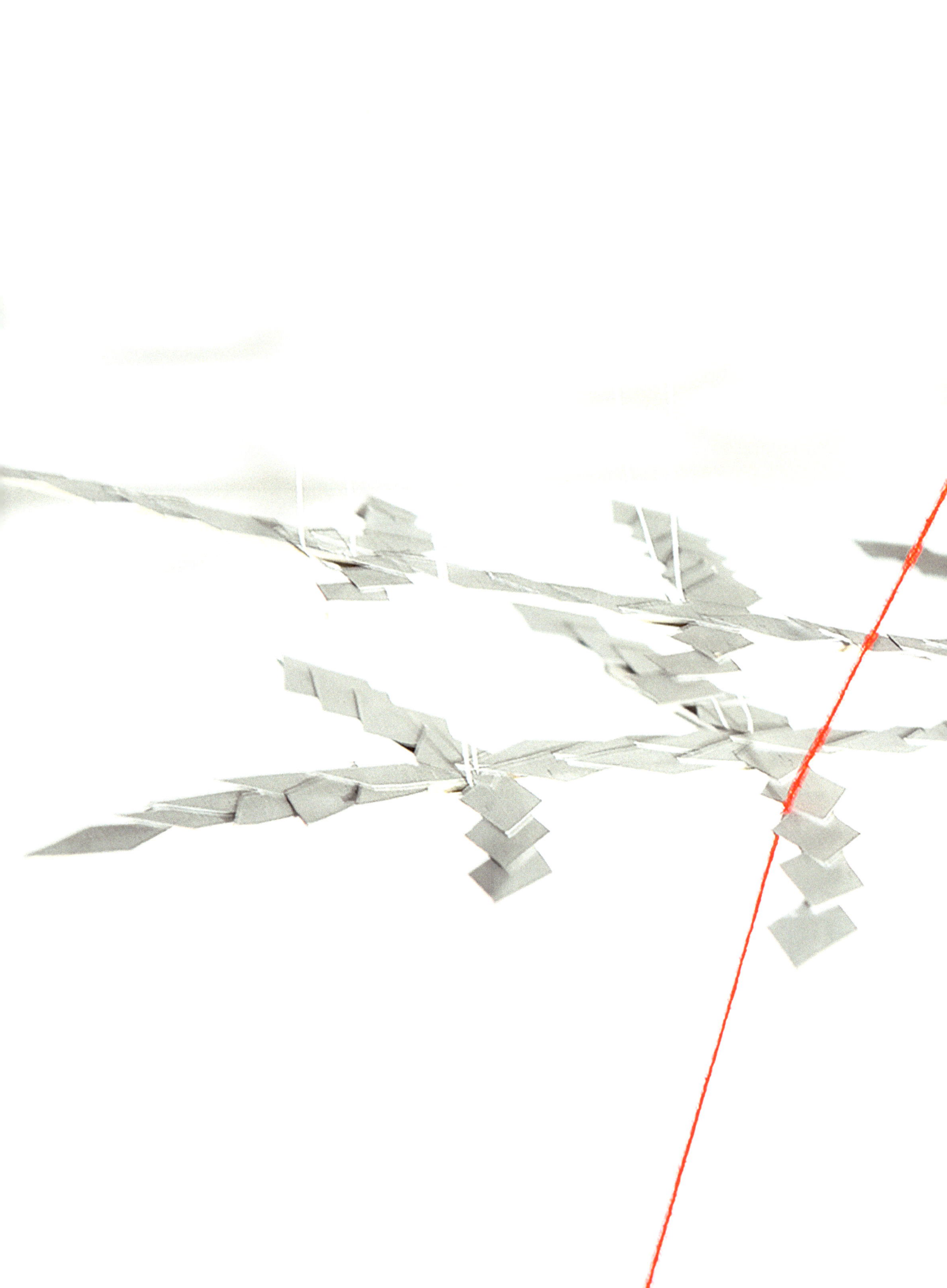

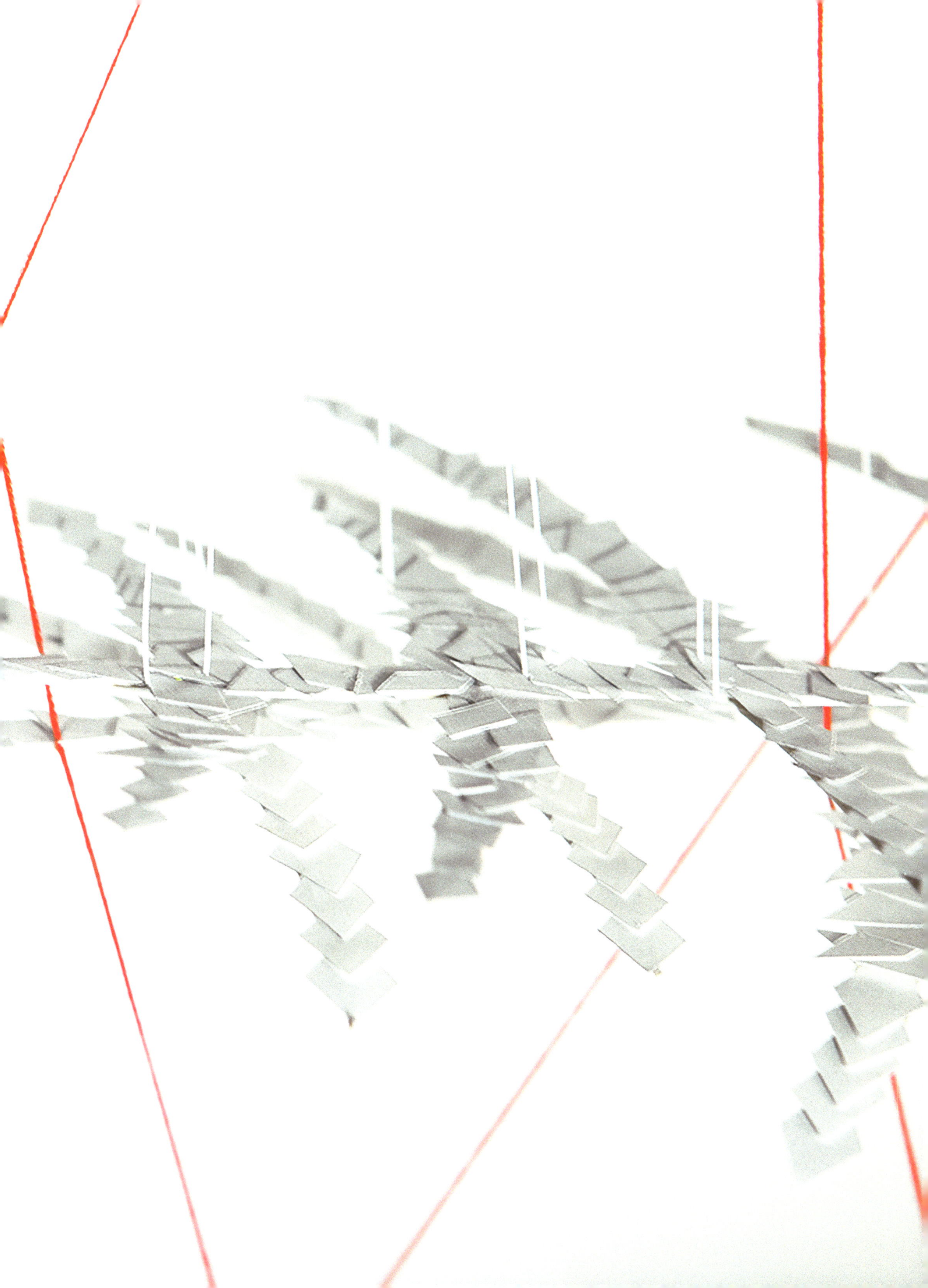

SYDNEY'S SHELLS

"Sydney's Shells," a project from my sophomore year studies in 3D art, was a study of the Sydney Opera House and the process and thought that created it. The project also sought to play with the battle between organic and structured design. Through creating this project I have found an intersection point between the two where great design exists.

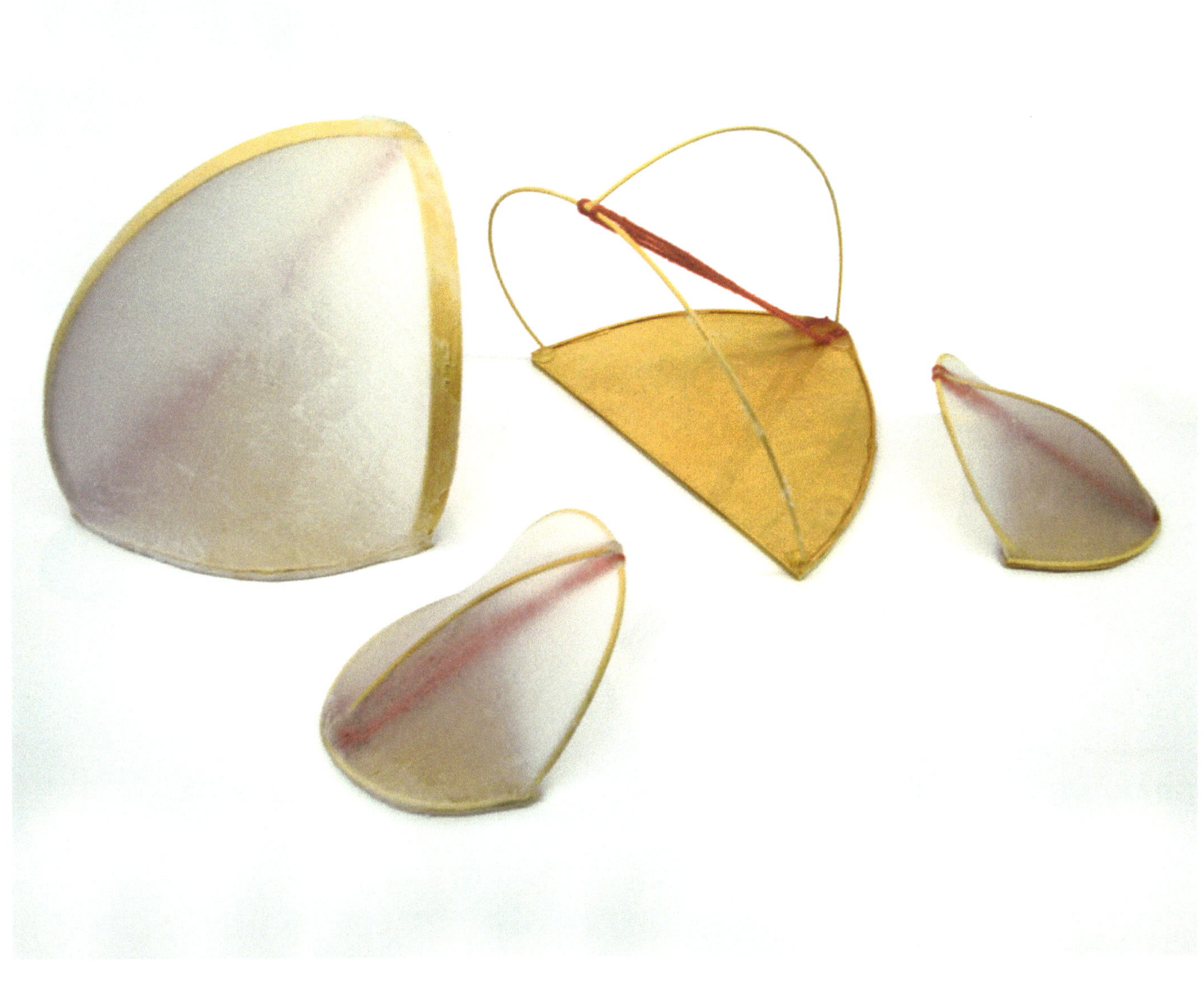

DRAWING

I know I draw without taking my pen off the page. I just keep going. I think of them as scribbles. I don't think they mean anything to anybody except to me, and then at the end of the day, the end of the project, they wheel out these little drawings and they're damn close to what the finished building is and it's the drawing...

Frank Gehry

LINES

An assignment from the second week of the Pratt PreCollege program in the summer of 2015. Students were instructed to draw various lines with varying spaces and angles. The project was an exercise in patience and attention to detail, and is one I will never forget.

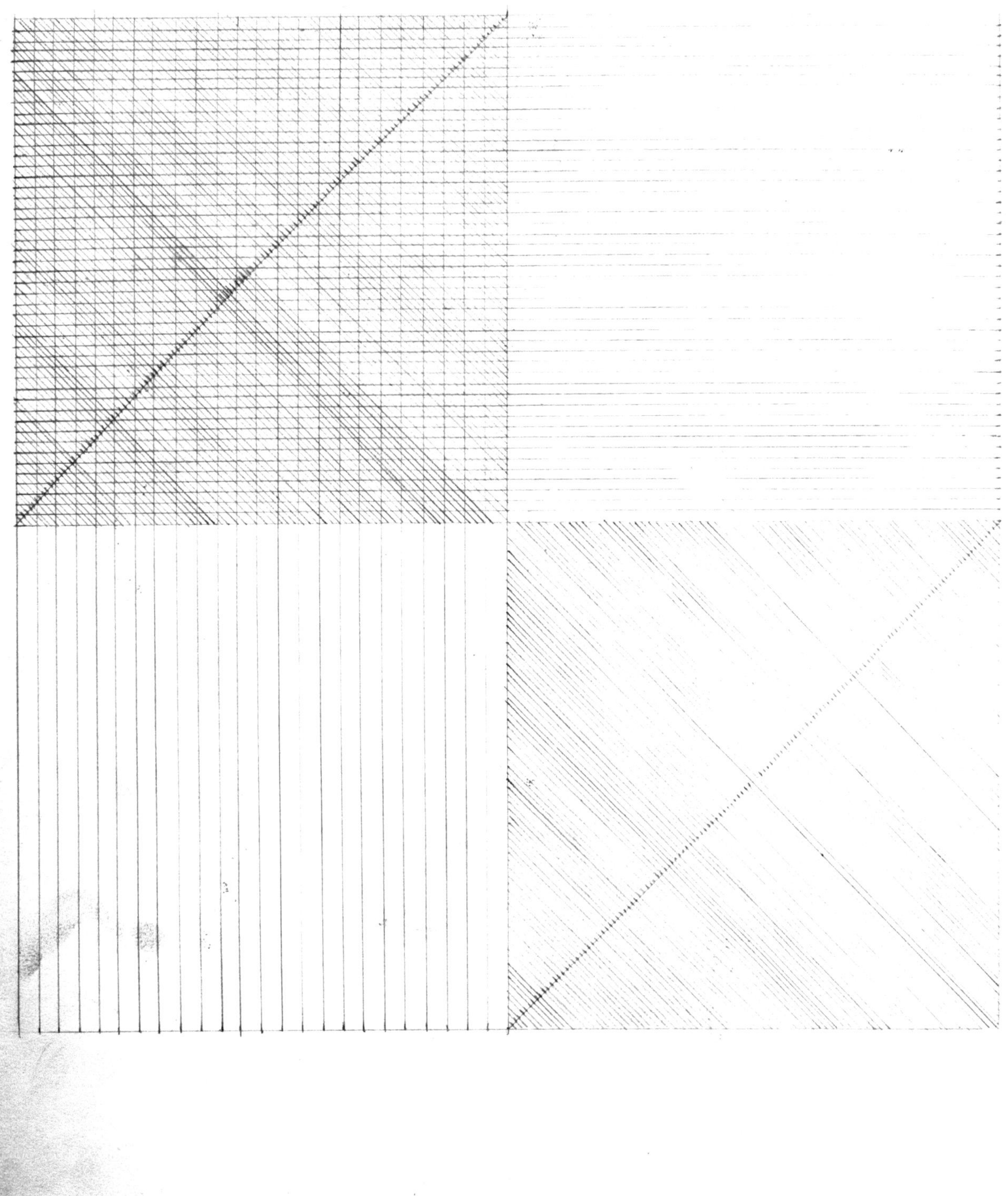

DEPTH CONCEPTIONS

Based upon Piet Mondrian's 1920 Composition No. II I took his planar work and extruded his composition. Keeping the same colors, the piece has a similar yet refreshing feel.

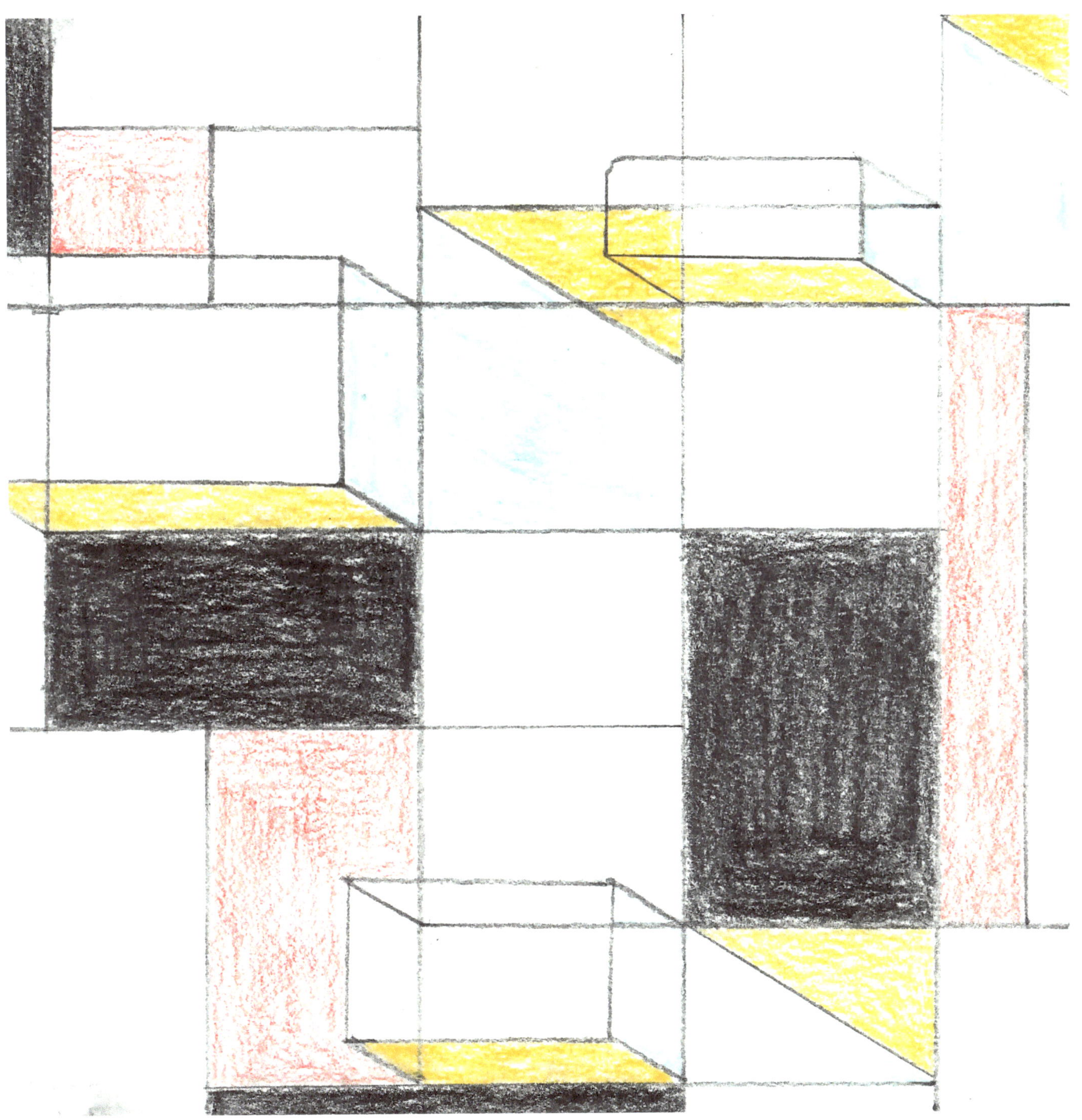

ONE BALA PLAZA

The "One Bala Plaza" drawings were created during my internship at Bohlin Cywinski Jackson in January of 2016. During my internship I was tasked with creating sketches of the new floor plan for the building.

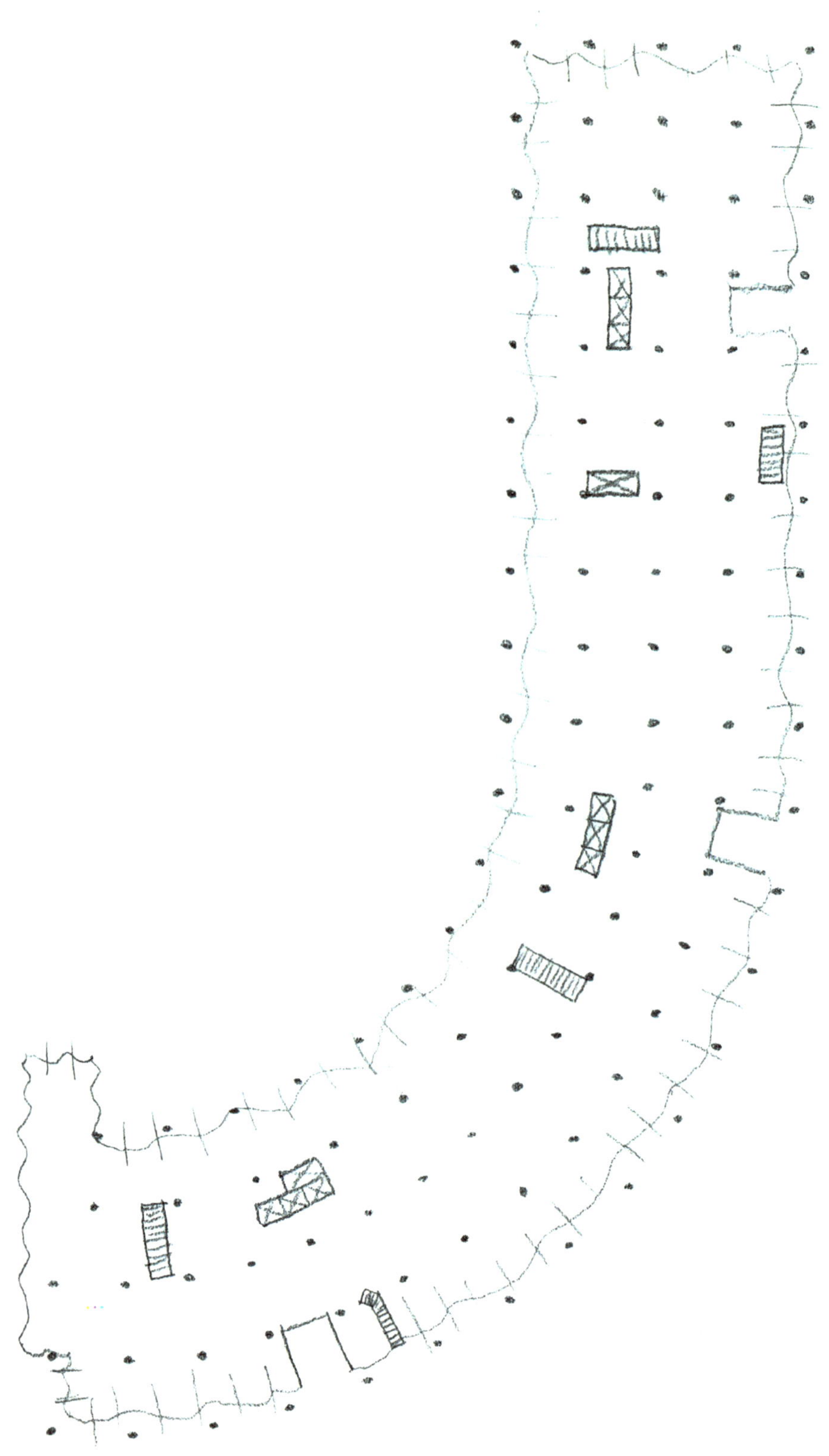

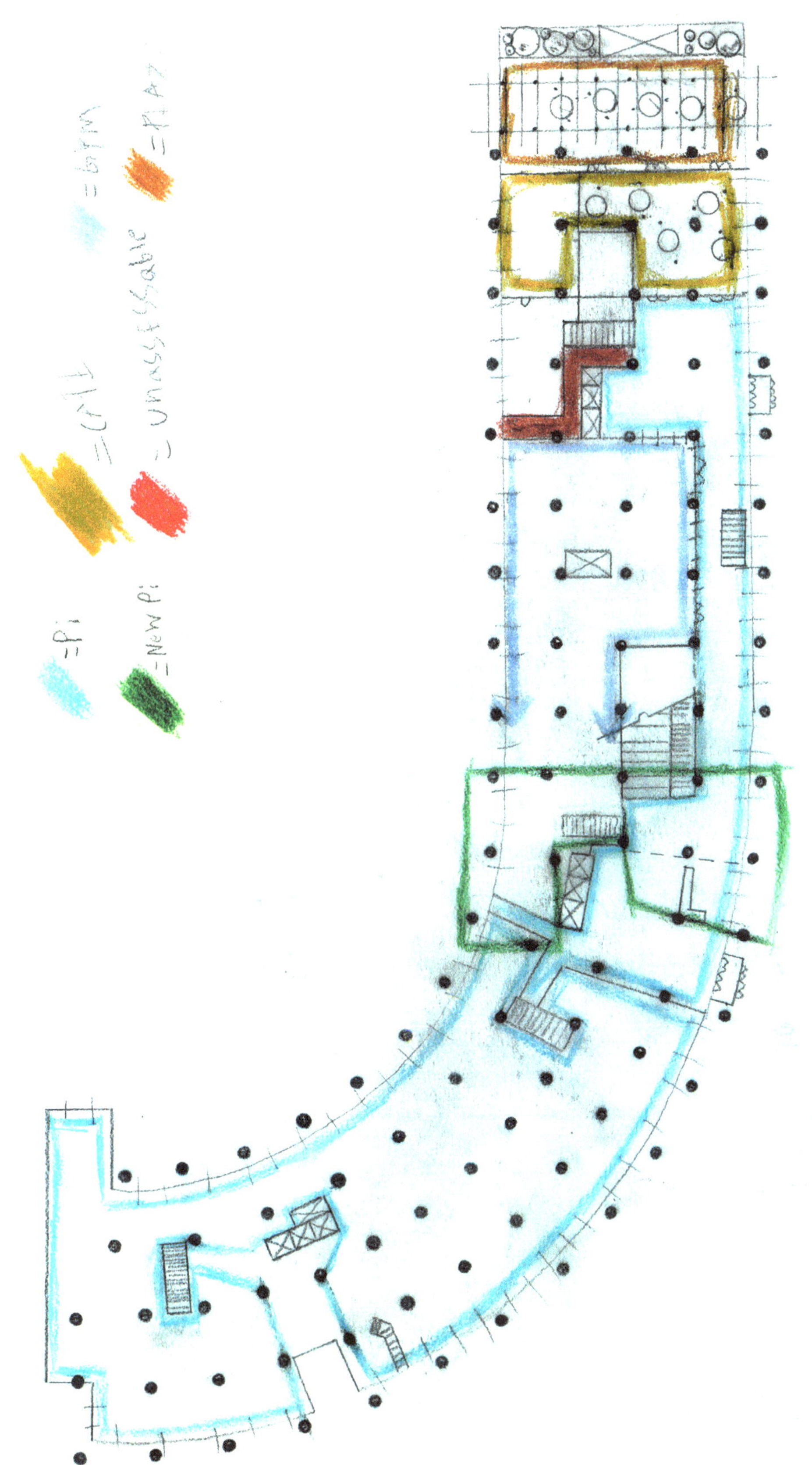
=Pi
=New Pi
=CAL
=Unassessable
=GYM

THE WOODLYNDE SCHOOL

The "Woodlynde School" drawings were created during my internship at Bohlin Cywinski Jackson in January of 2016. During my internship I was tasked with creating sketches of the existing floor plan of the school to help the clients better understand their building.

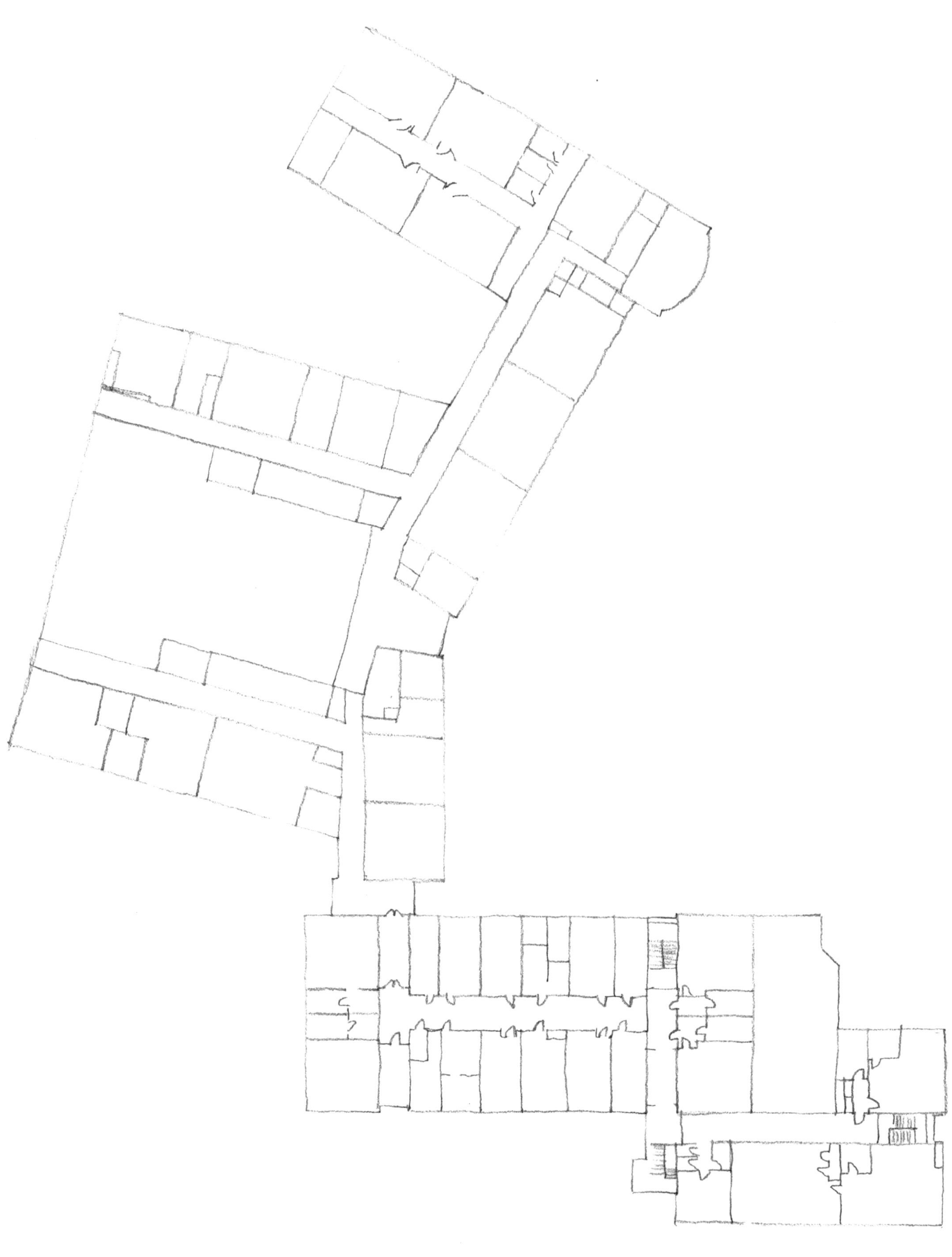

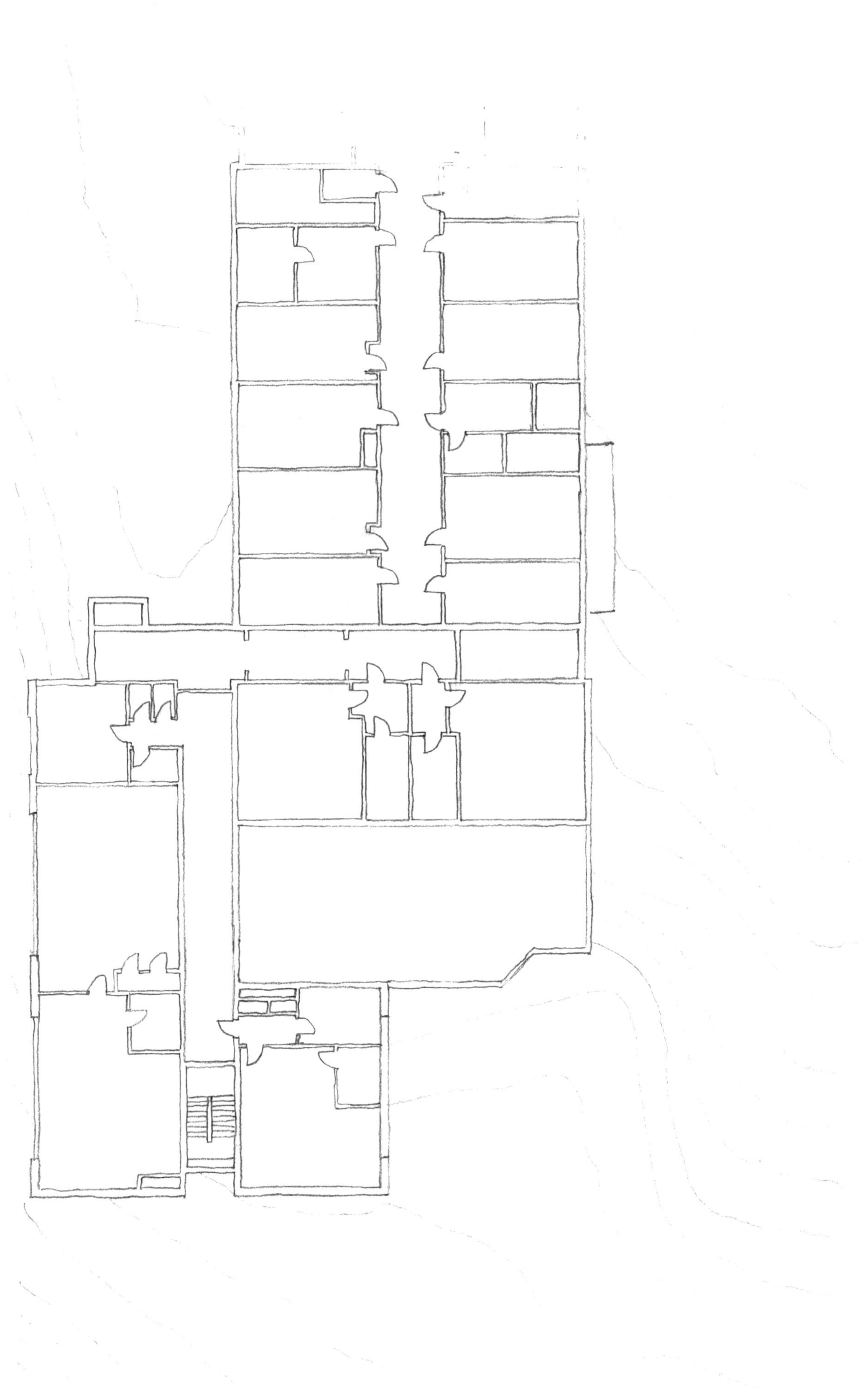

FIGURE DRAWING

From my senior year art studio course, we spent three nights drawing the nude form. The drawings are expressive, gestural, quick, and raw.

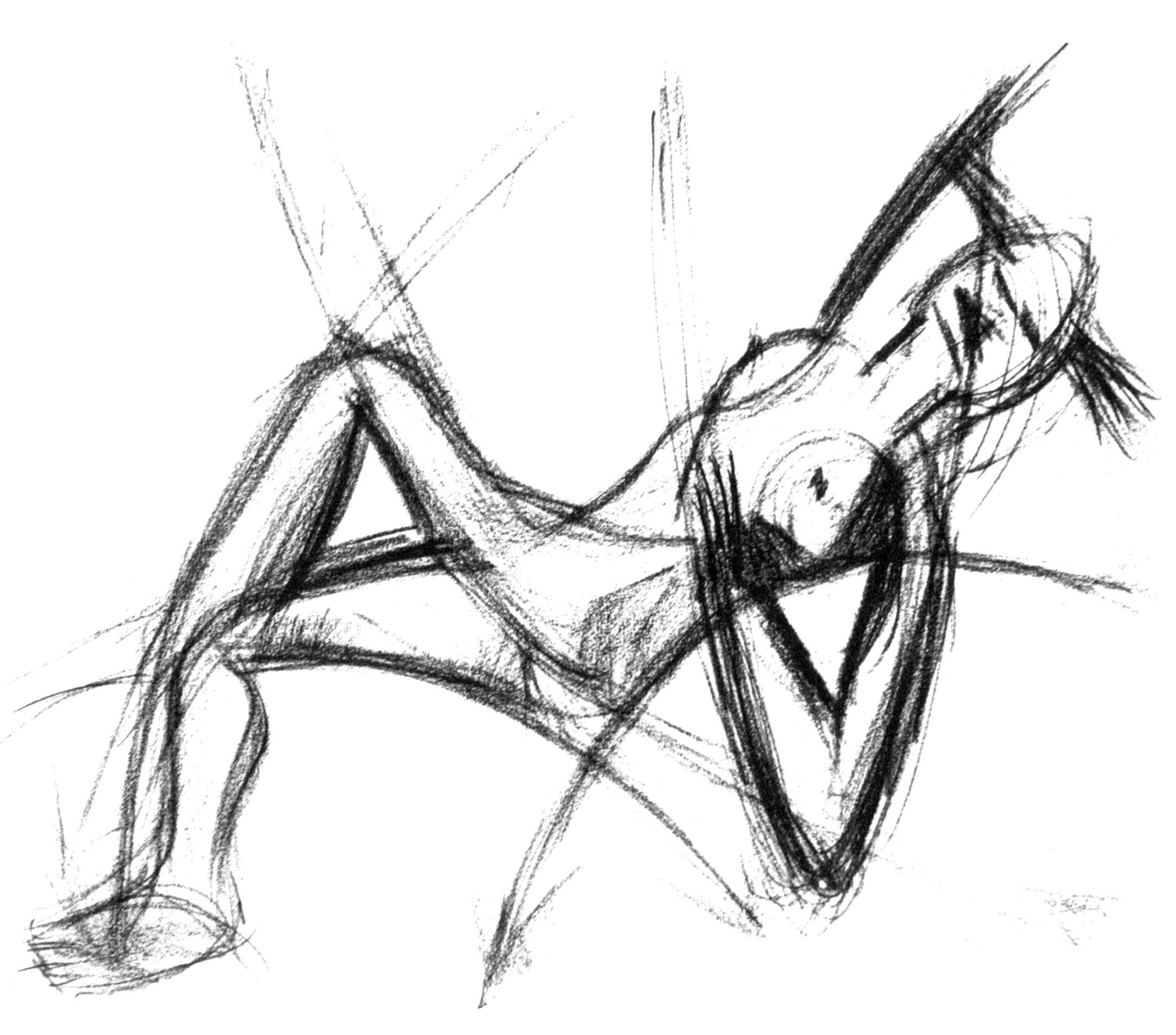

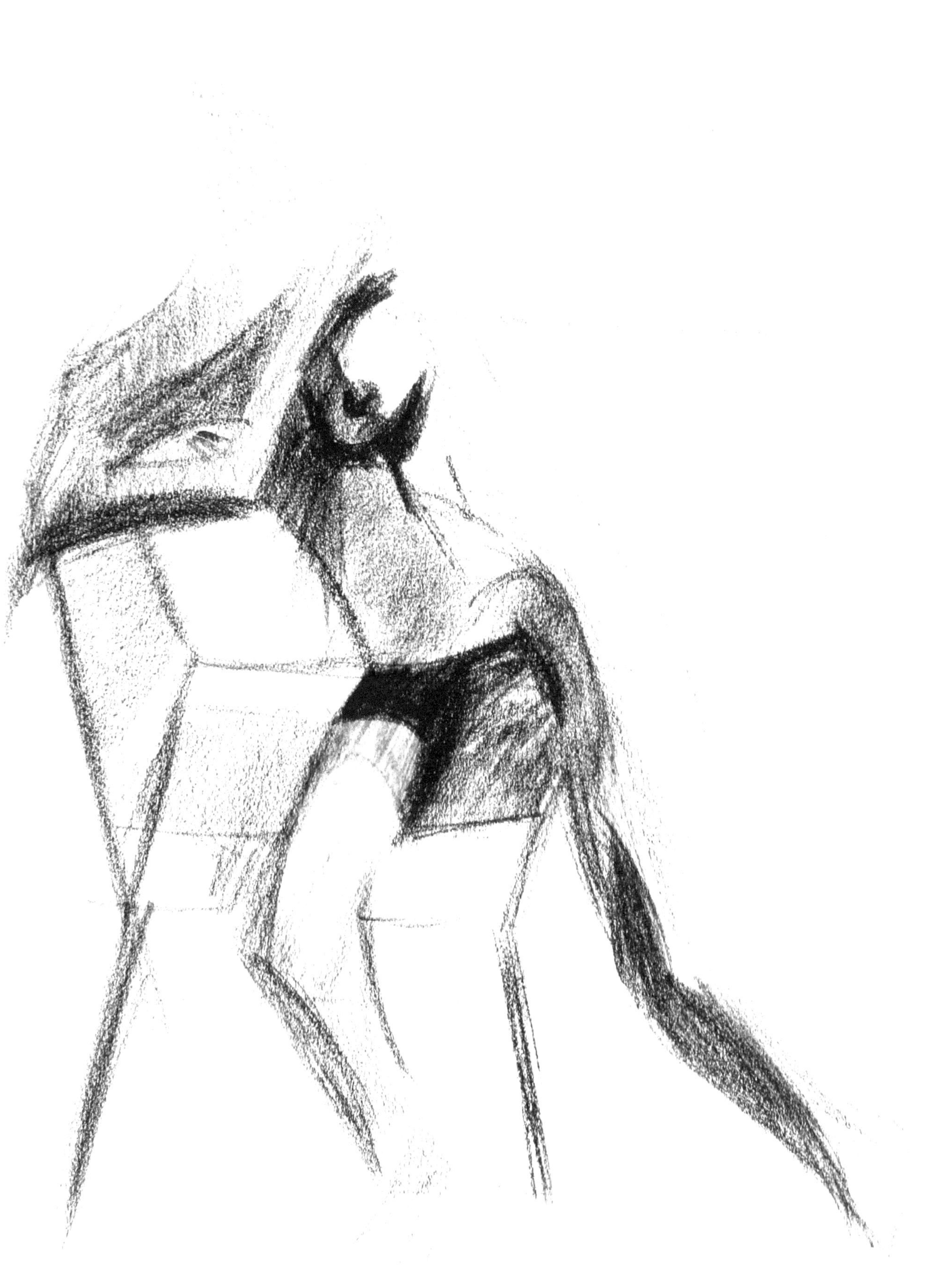

DESIGN

True simplicity is, well, you just keep on going and going until you get to the point where you go, "Yeah, well, of course." Where there's no rational alternative.

Jonathan Ive

PESTER

A collage from Color & Design in my junior year, based on the word pester. Each square seeks to define pester in a different way, some employing color, shape, and scale to visually define the word.

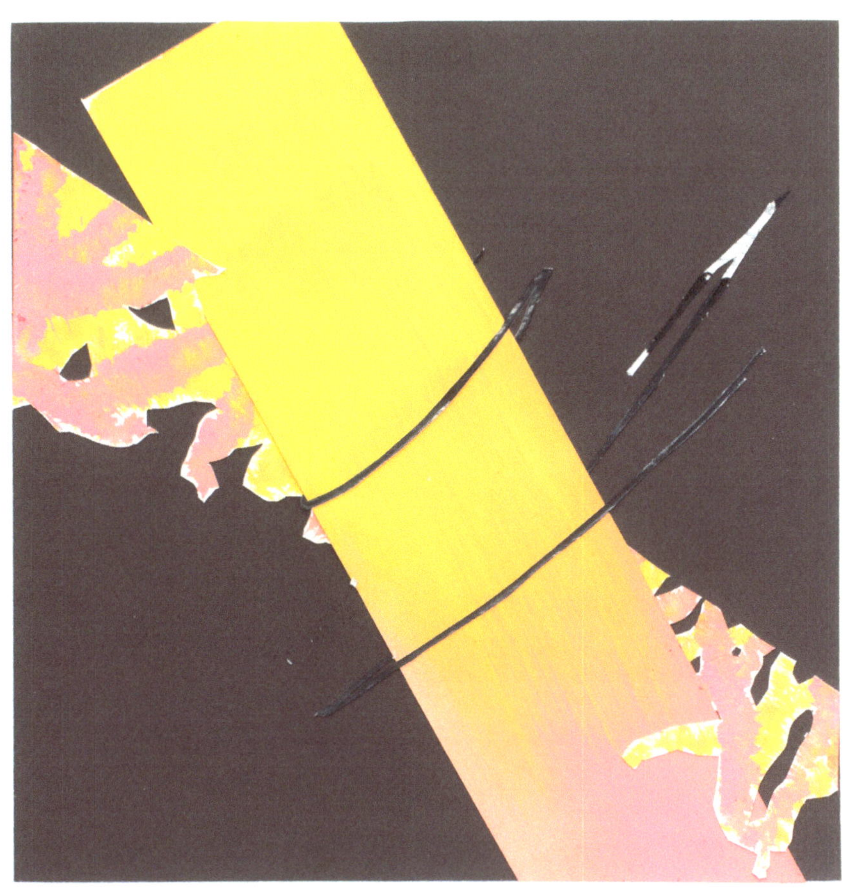

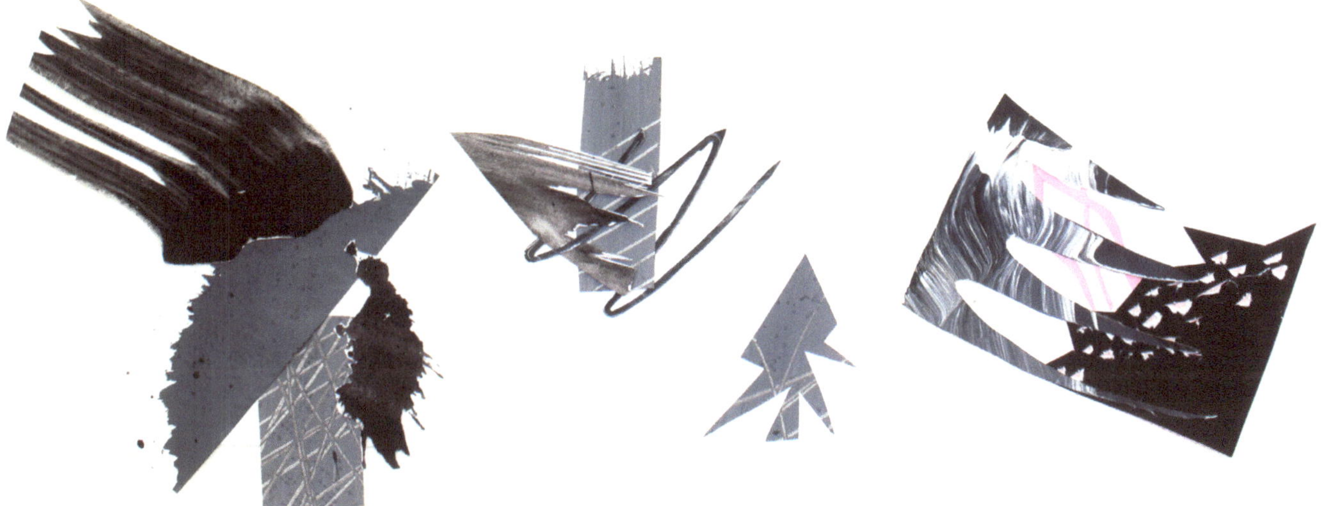

PROCEDURAL DRAWING: OBJECT / ENVIRONMENT

From a digital collage my senior year, this procedural drawing was designed as part of a project on the object versus the environment. One cell was designed by hand and then replicated, repeated, warped and skewed in Illustrator using scripts.

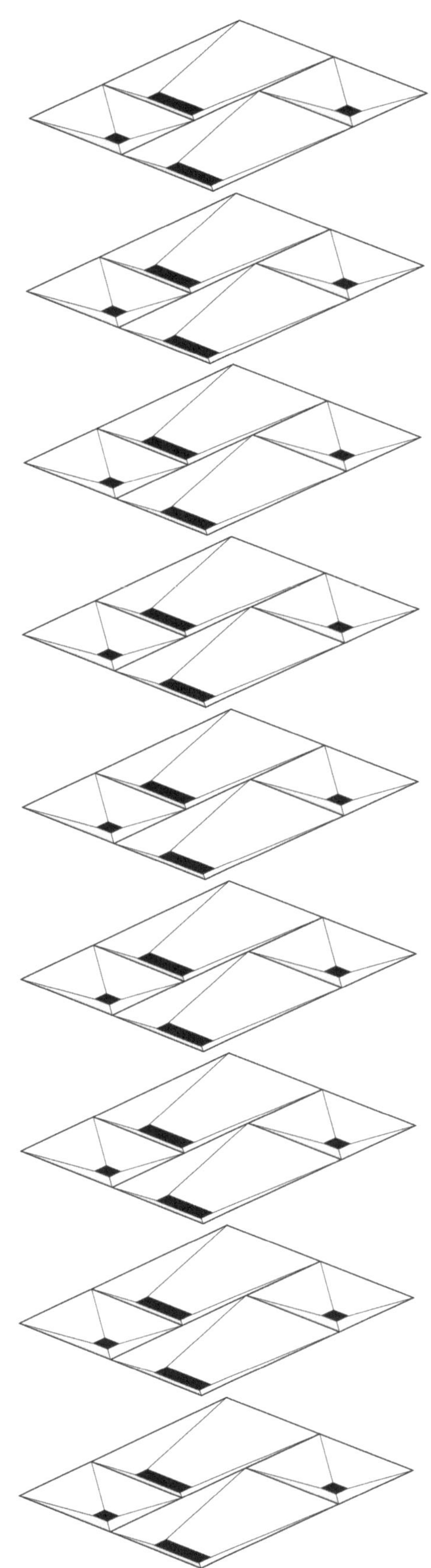

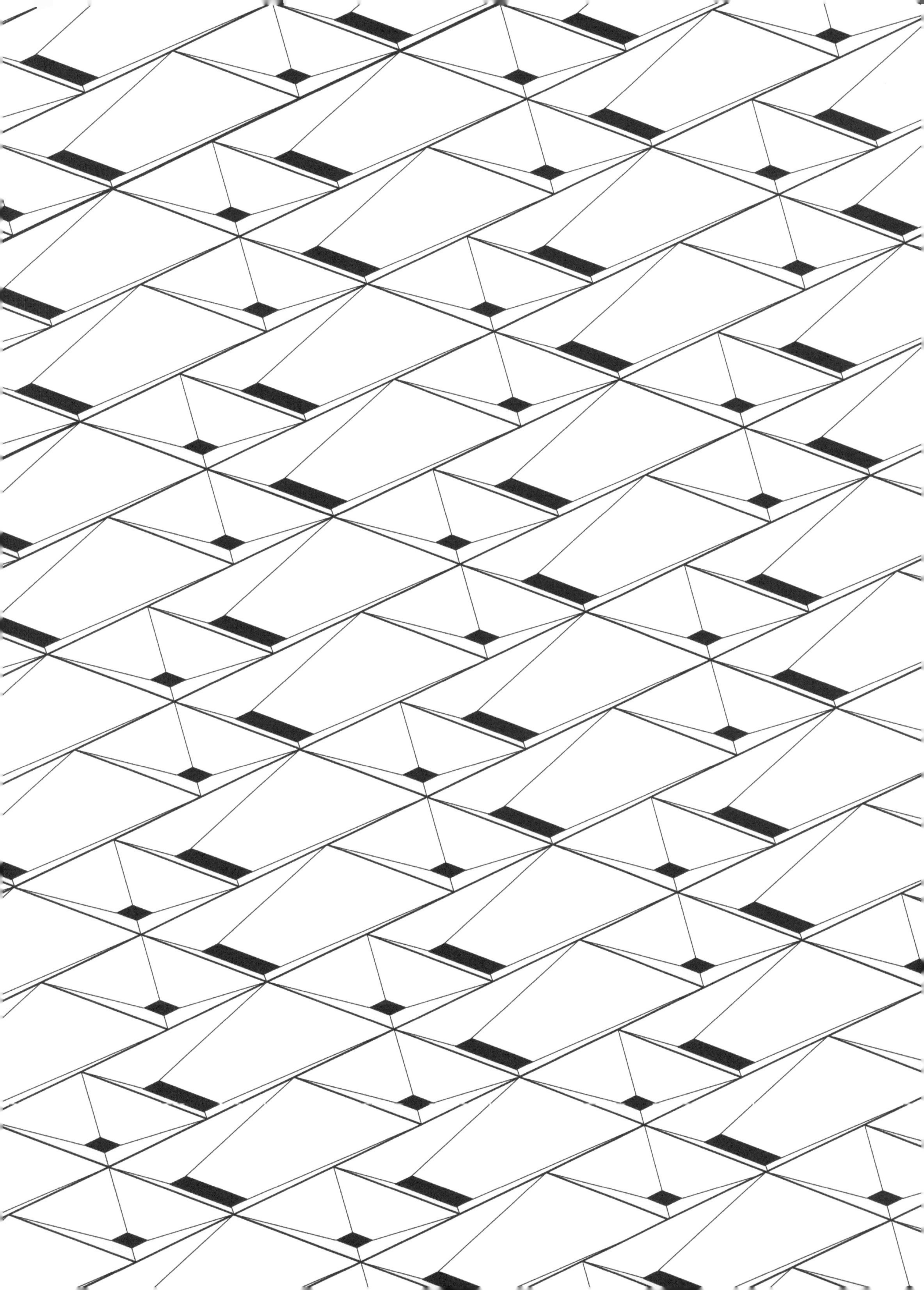

SENTENCE ILLUMINATION

Created for my senior English course, I selected an excerpt of George Orwell's *1984* and fleshed it out. This project revolves around highlighting and suppressing major and minor concepts from the excerpt as *1984*'s The Party does.

To the future or to the past, to a time when thought is free, when **men are different** from one another and **do not live alone**—to a time when **truth exists** and what is **done cannot be undone:**

from the age of **uniformity,**

from the age of **solitude,**

from the age of **Big Brother,**

from the age of **doublethink**

—greetings!

MOUNT FUJI

Creating "Mount Fuji," I worked in Adobe Photoshop, creating, layering, and warping texture images. The project is based on the iconic view of Mount Fuji in Japan. I took photographs and scanned in textures to layer above this image to create a new unique and more abstract piece. My final image is composed solely of layered textures.

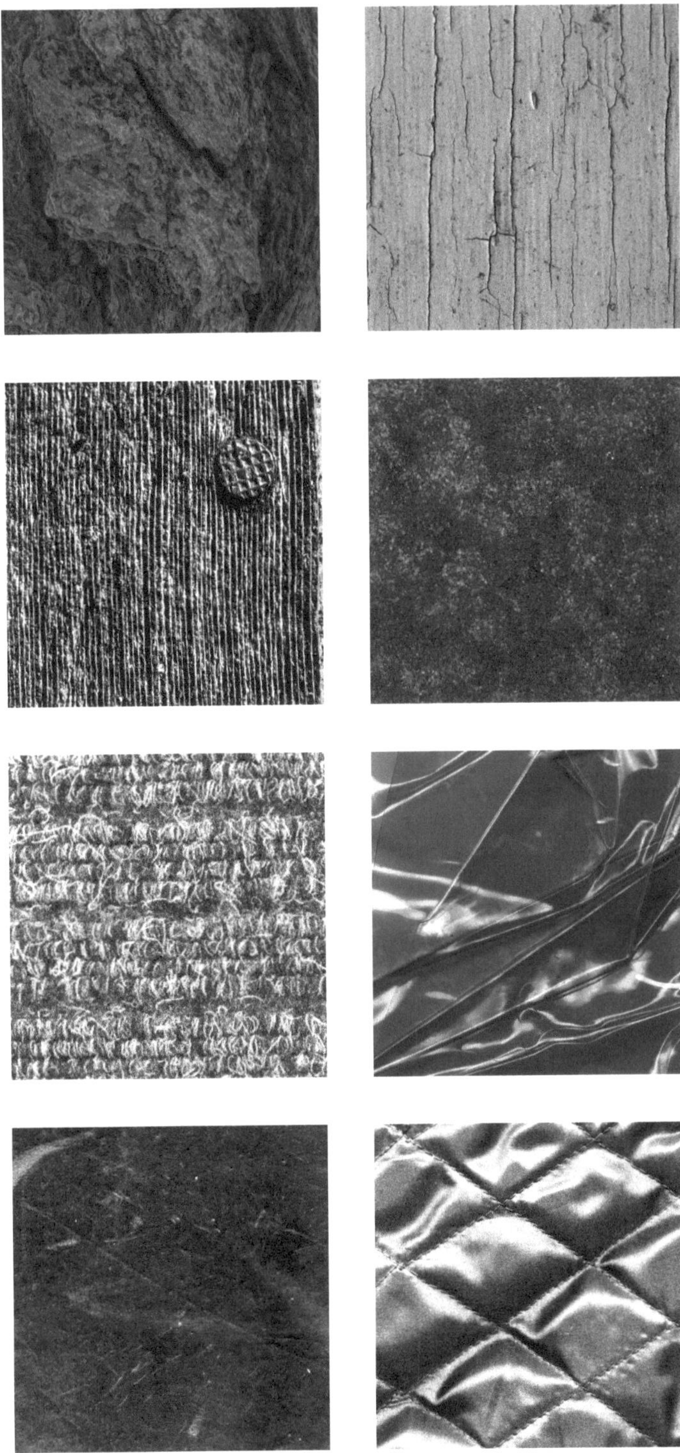

PAINTING

The object of art is not to reproduce reality, but to create a reality of the same intensity.

Alberto Giacometti

LETTERS AS SHAPES

This project is from my freshman year Foundation course. The piece is composed of varying overlaid letters to create mysterious shapes that maintain their detectability as letters.

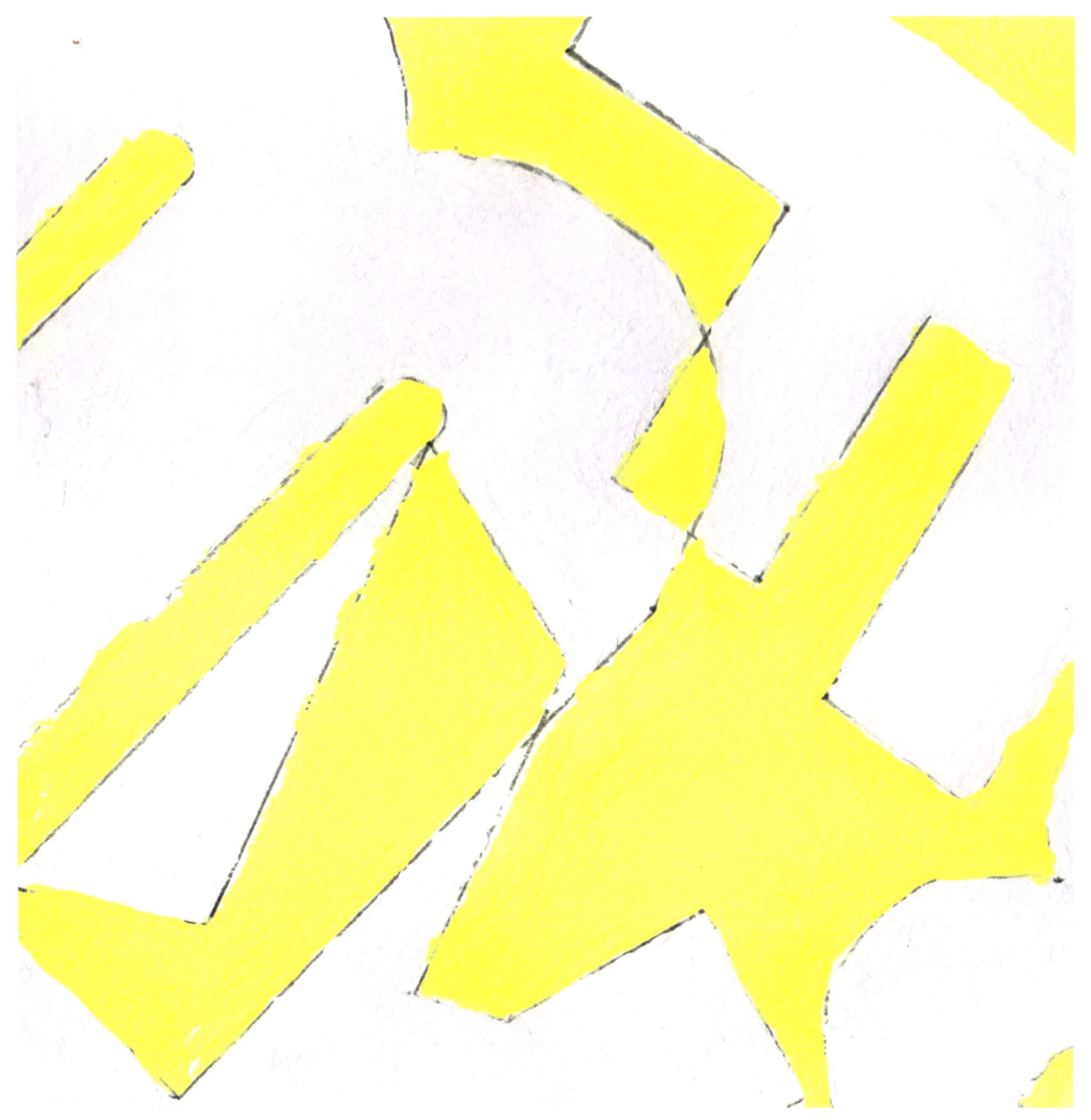

SIXTY SECOND PAINTINGS

A series of sixty second paintings based on a historical landscape painting. This project was completed in Senior Studio at the end of 2016. I used black paint and a dry brush to add texture and depth to the project within a short period of time.

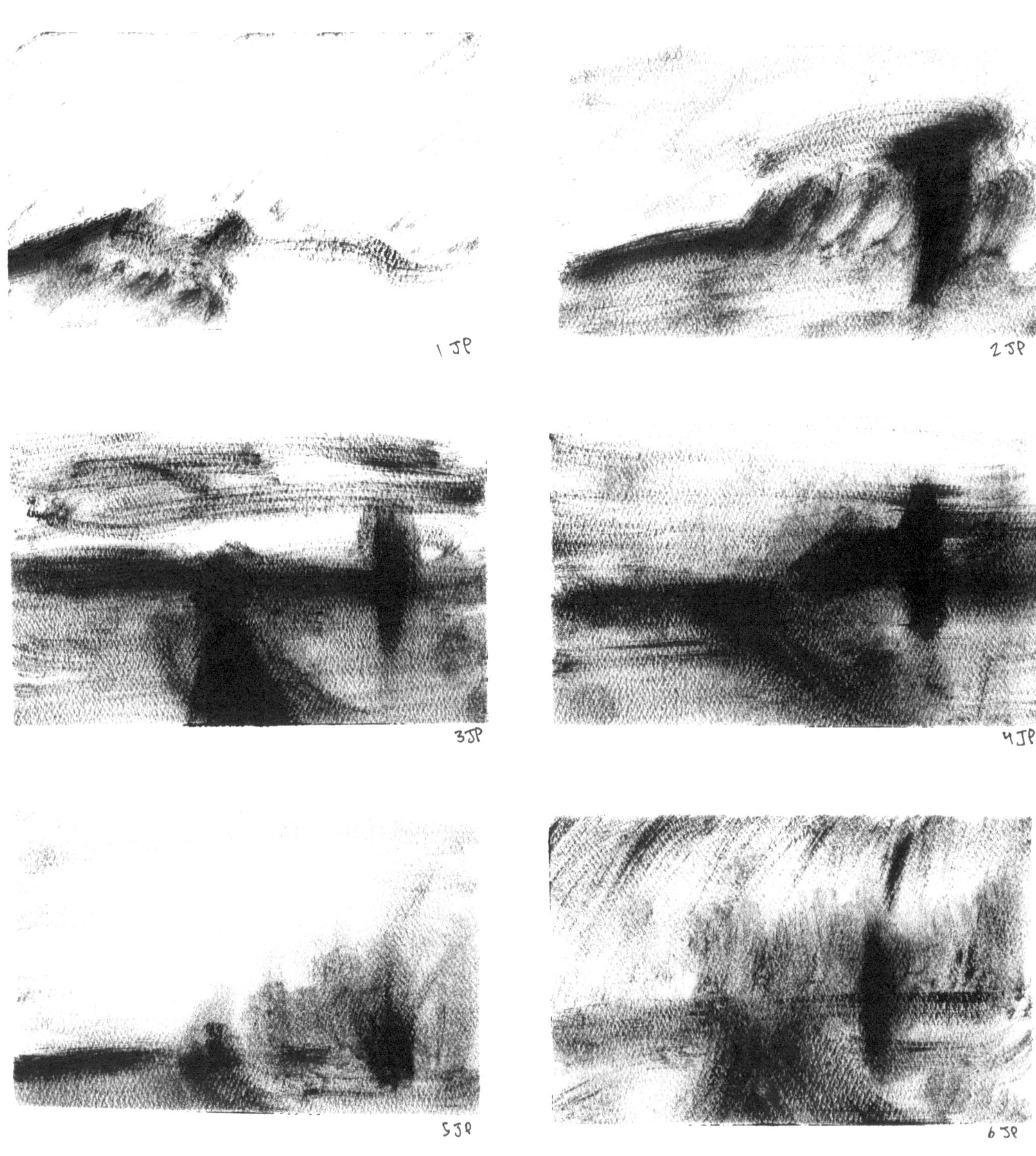
1 JP
2 JP
3JP
4JP
5JP
6 JP

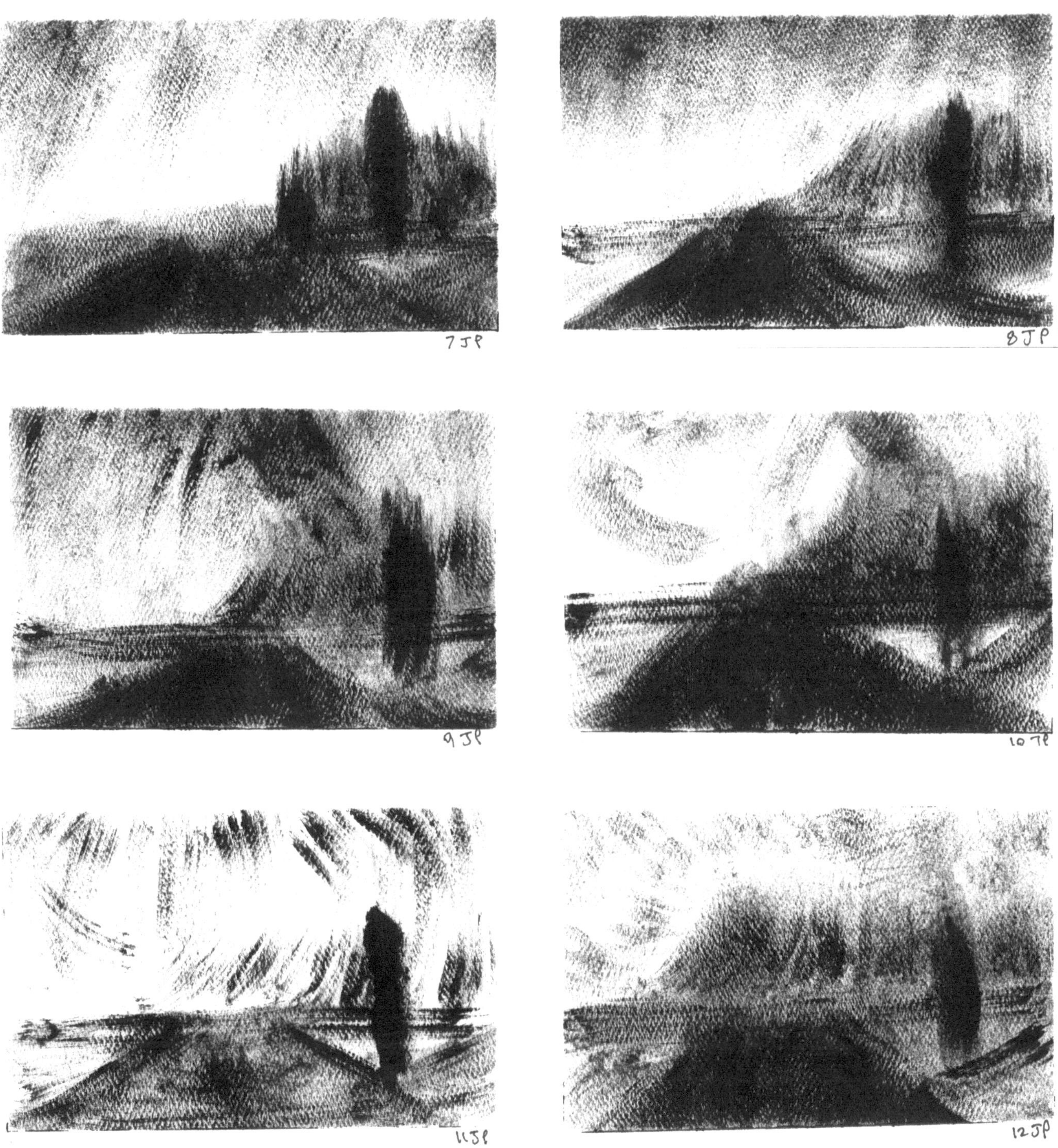
7 JP
8 JP
9 JP
10 JP
11 JP
12 JP

A MAN IN A HAT

"A Man in a Hat" was a Color & Design project created in my junior year. The project assignment was to create an abstraction using a different color palette than the original work. I chose to work from Piero della Francesca's portraits of Federico da Montefeltro.

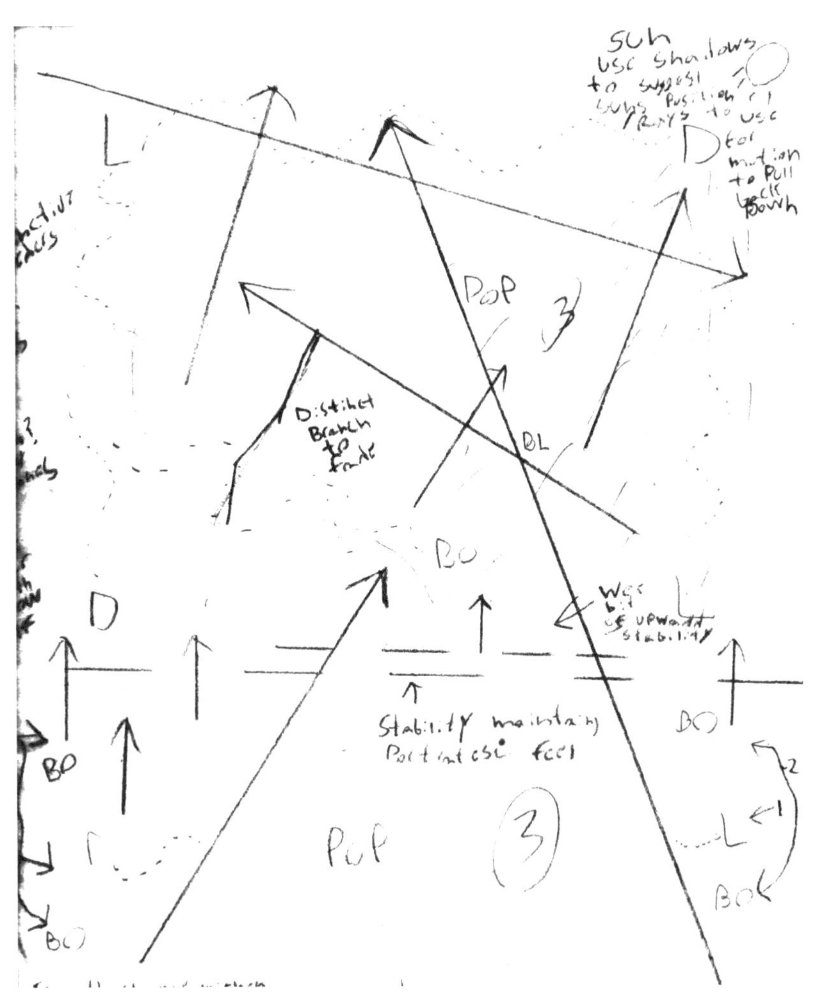
Sun
L
D
PoP
3
Distinct Branch to frame
BL
BO
D
Stability maintain
PoP
3
L
BO

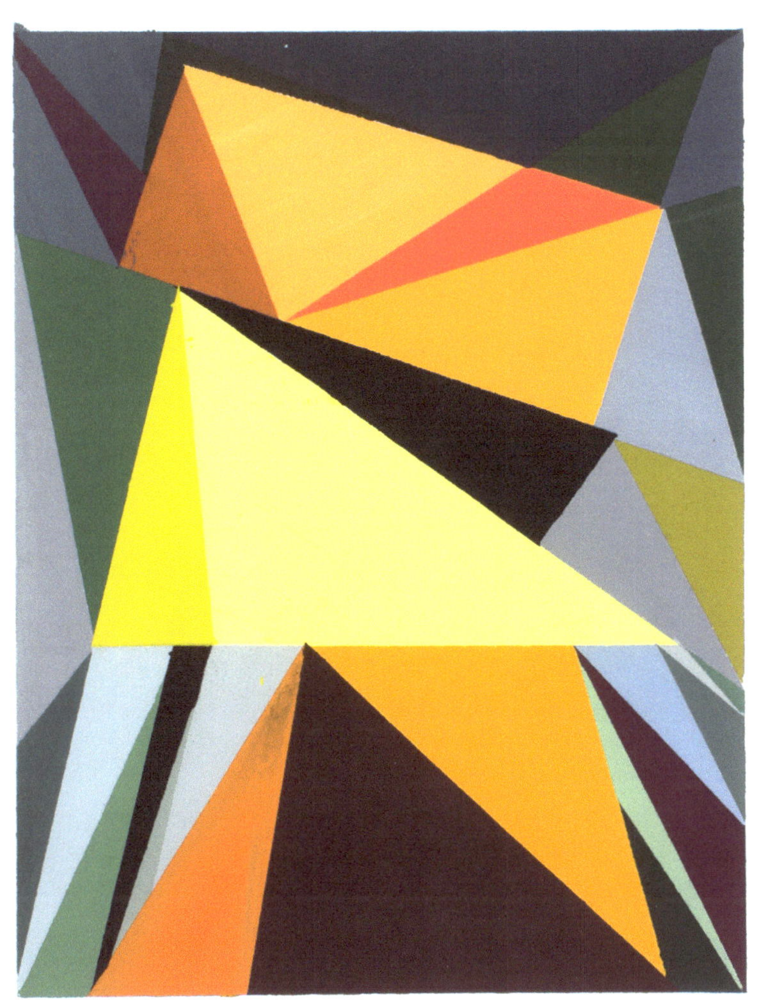

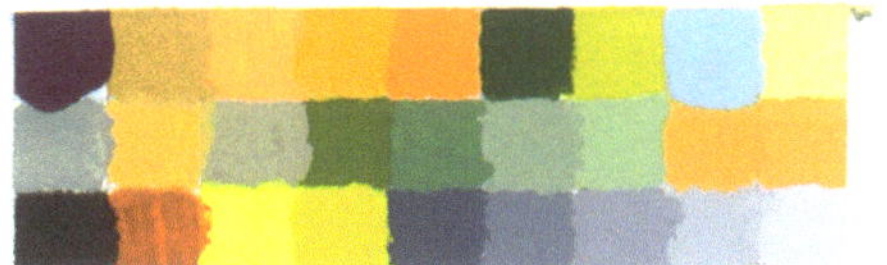

DRIPPING

This painting was created using water and spray paint. The painting is on a 15" × 20" piece of art board. During the making of this piece, I propped the piece of board up outside and began by pouring water down the board. Simultaneously, I sprayed varying colors of paint into the water and watched them drip across the canvas.

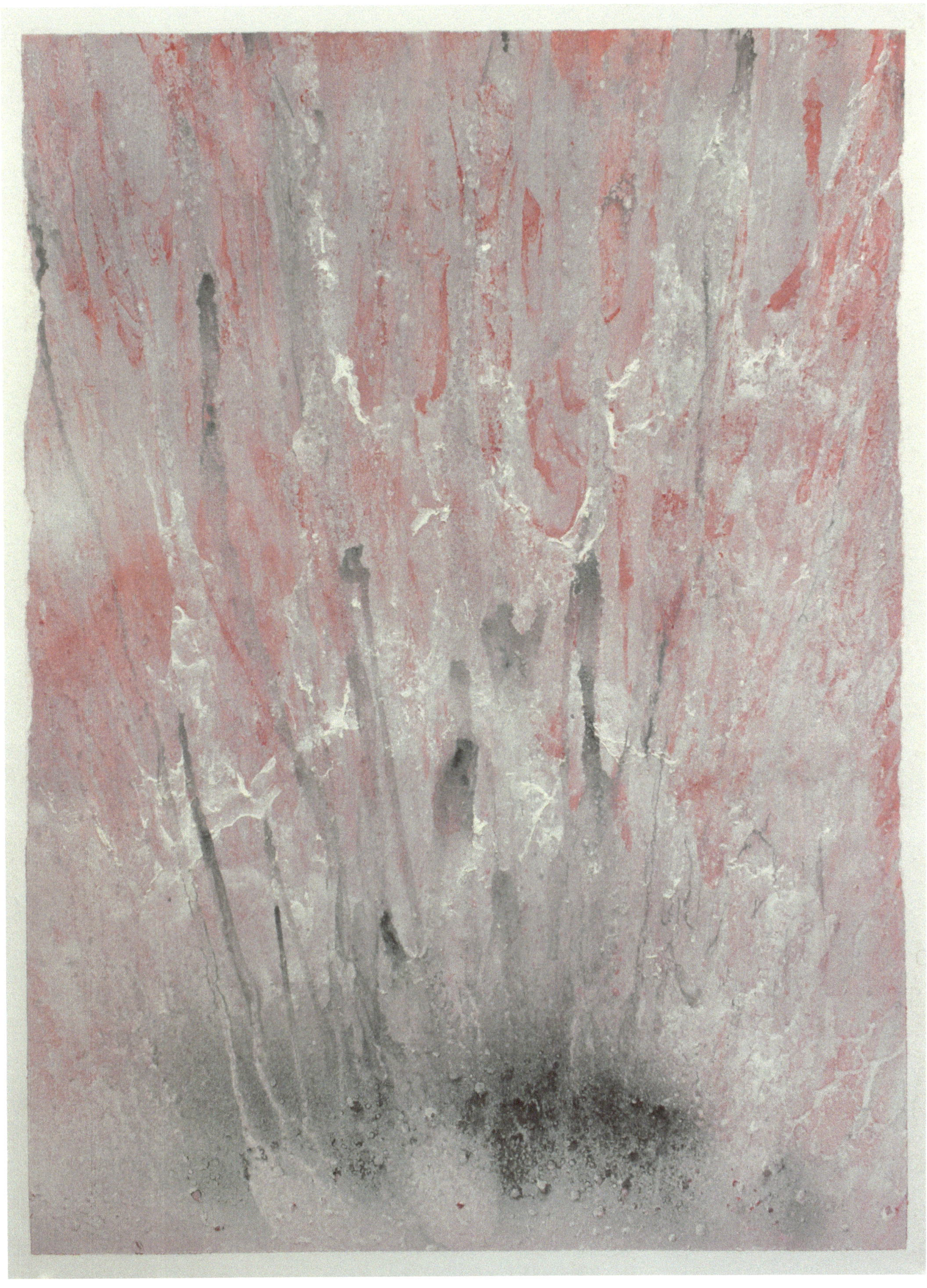

SELF-PORTRAIT

This self-portrait was created in Color & Design during the spring of 2016. The project was inspired by Andy Warhol's portraits of Mao.

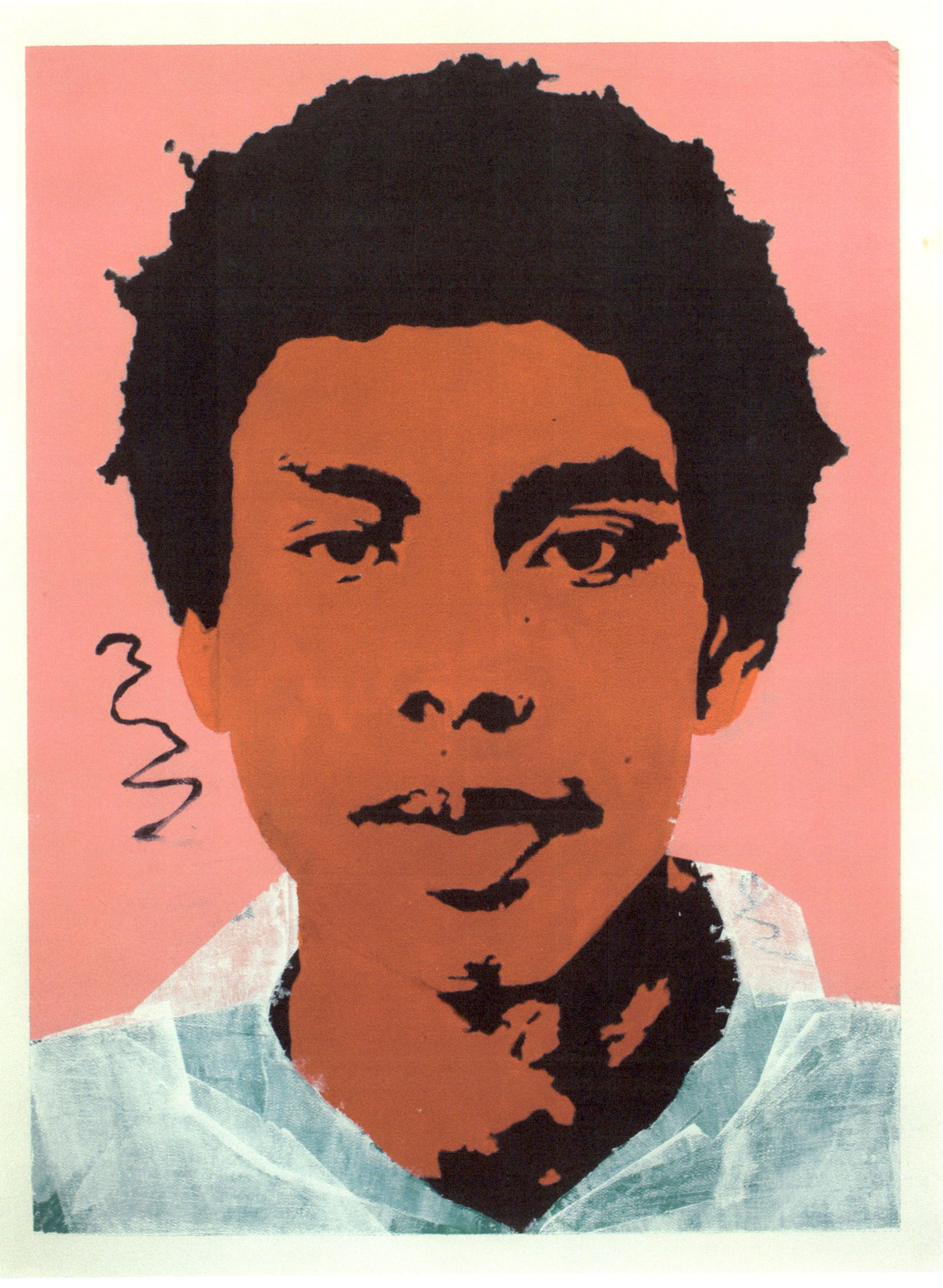

PHOTOGRAPHY

My preference for clear structures is the result of my desire—perhaps illusory—to keep track of things and maintain my grip on the world.

Andreas Gursky

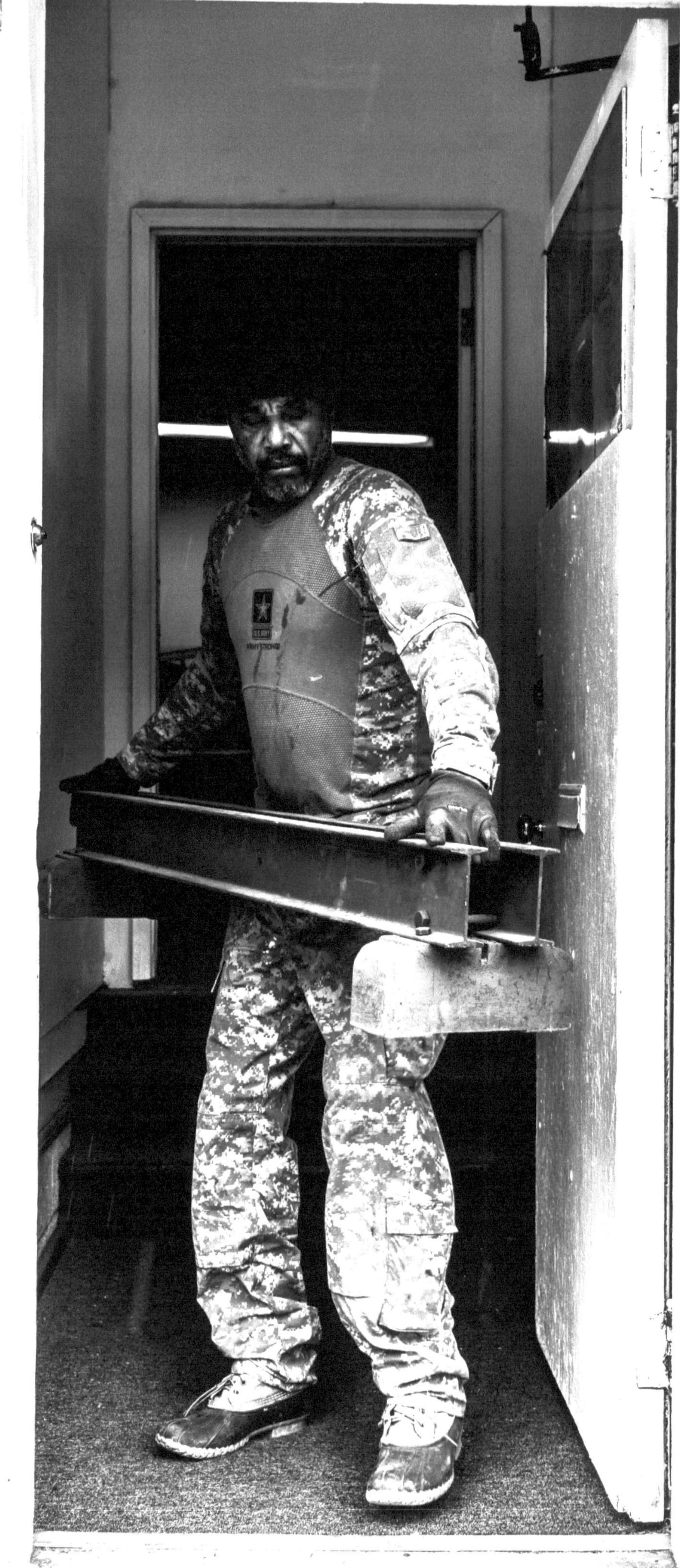
ARMY STRONG

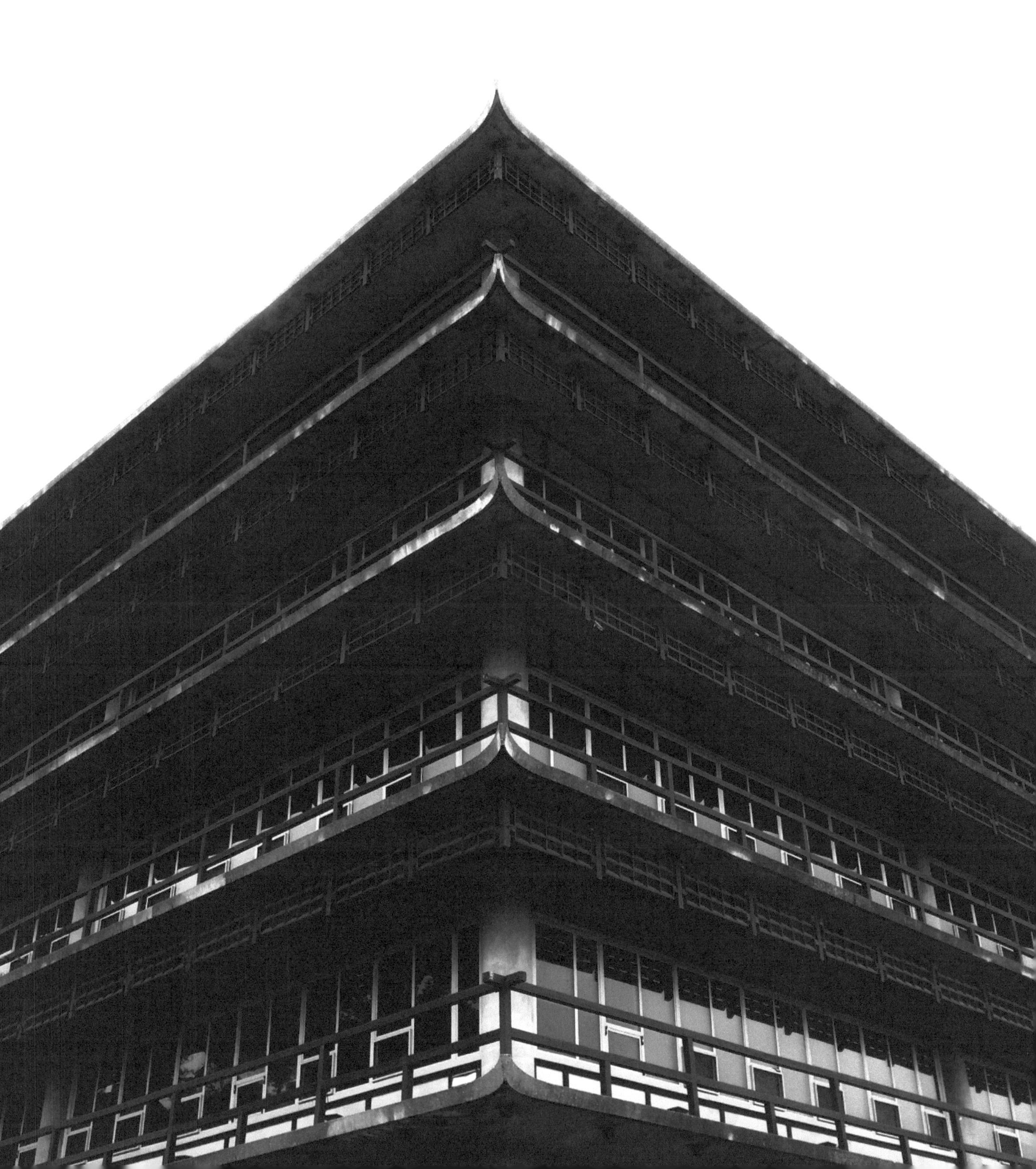

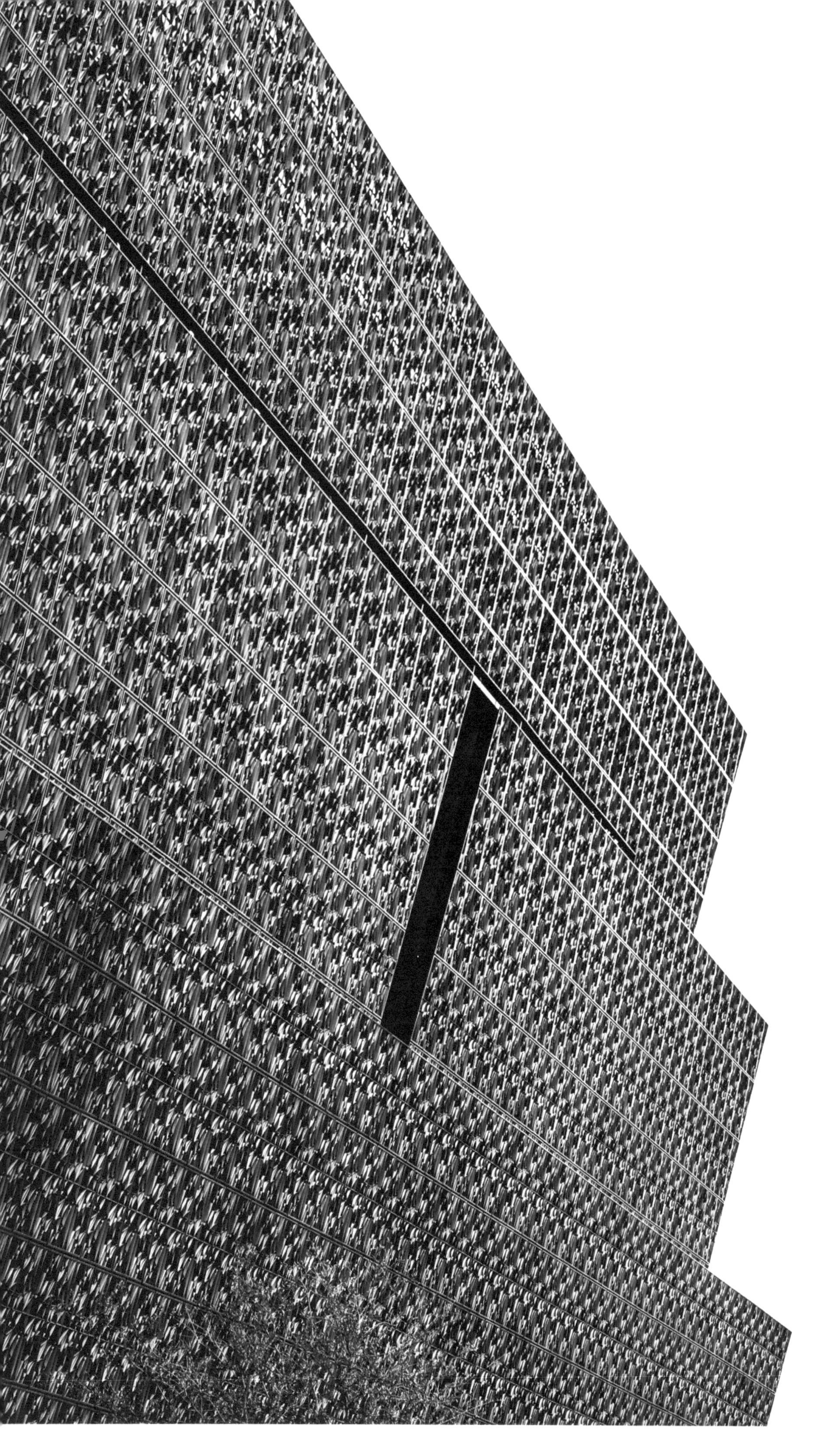

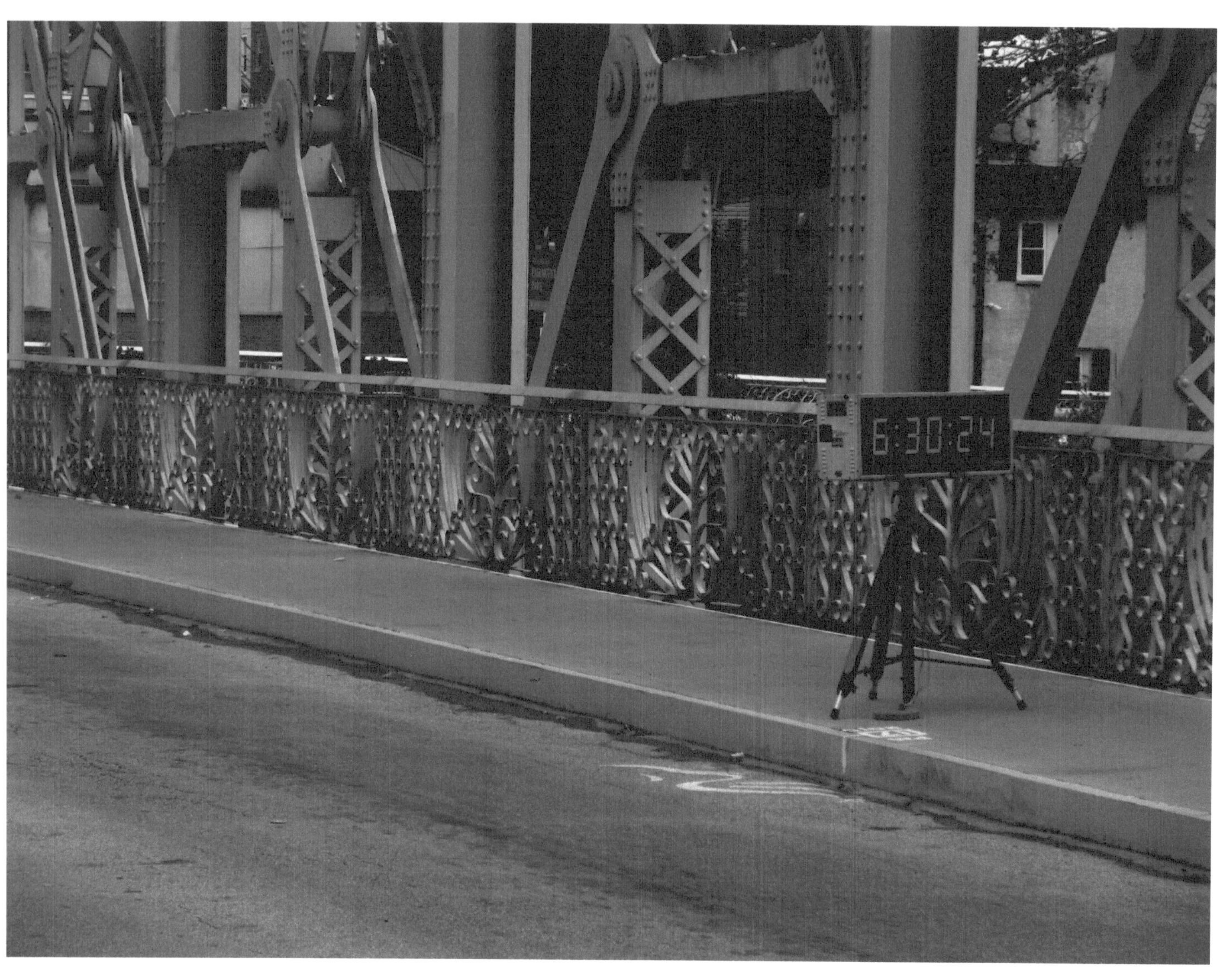
6:30:24

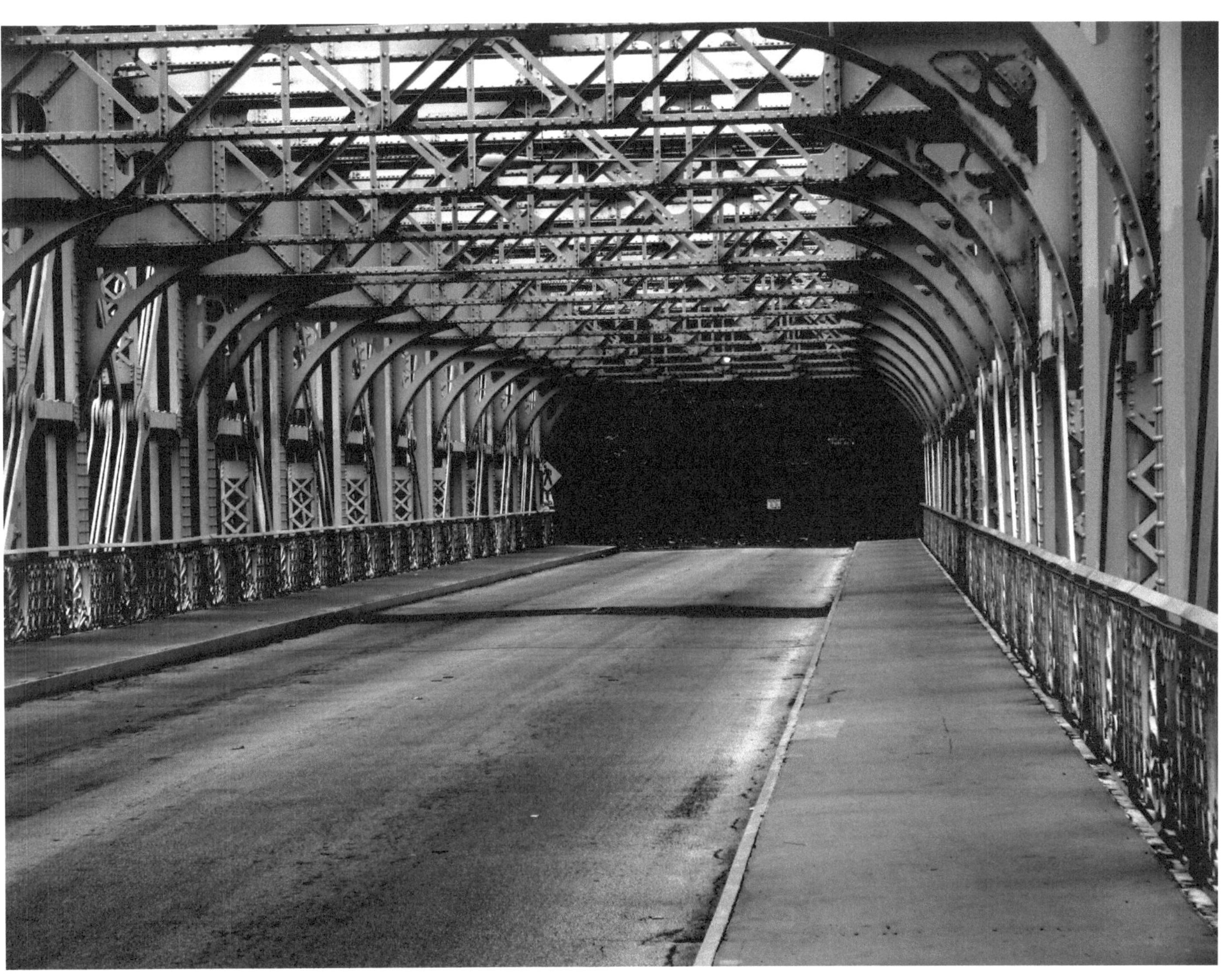

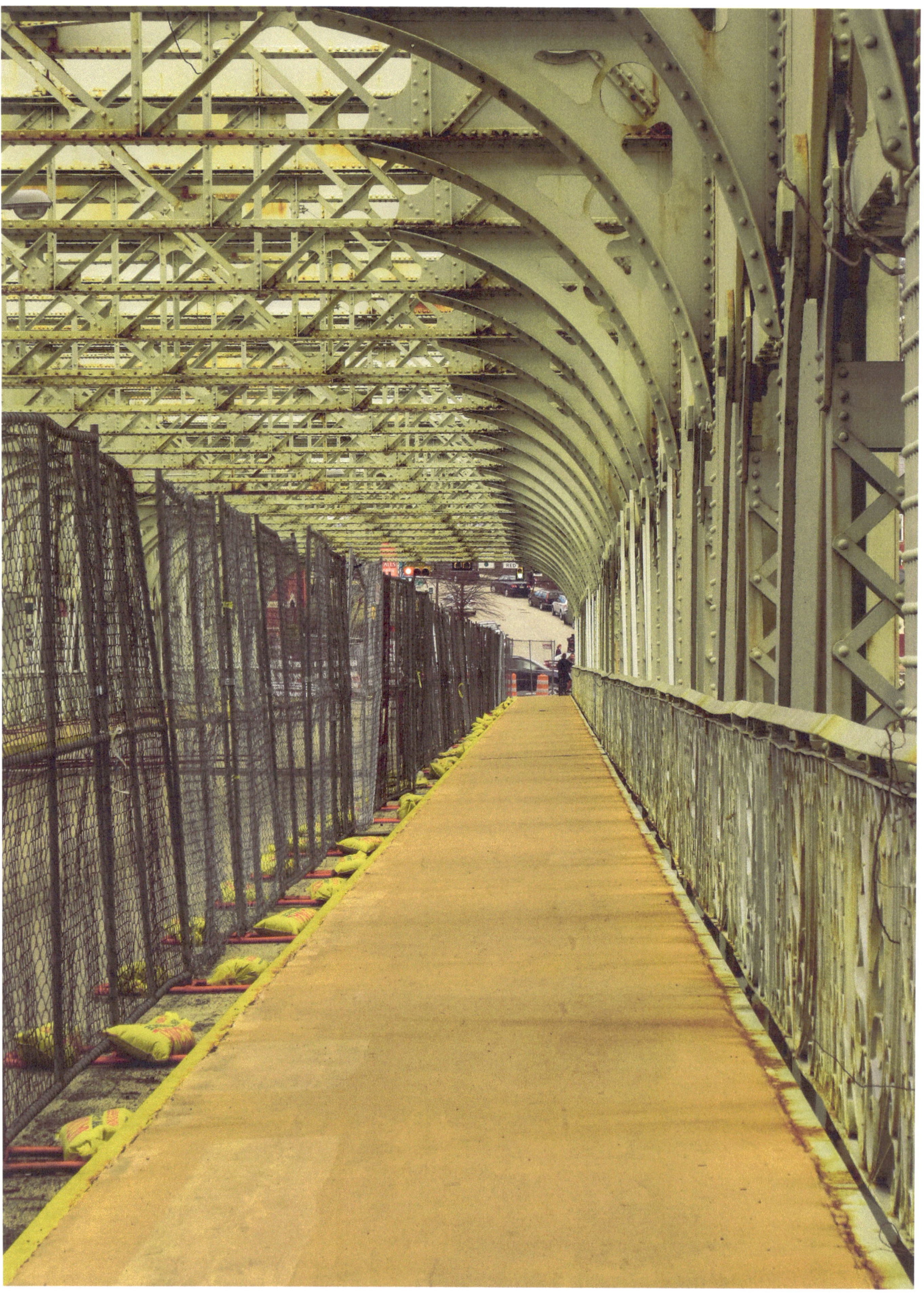

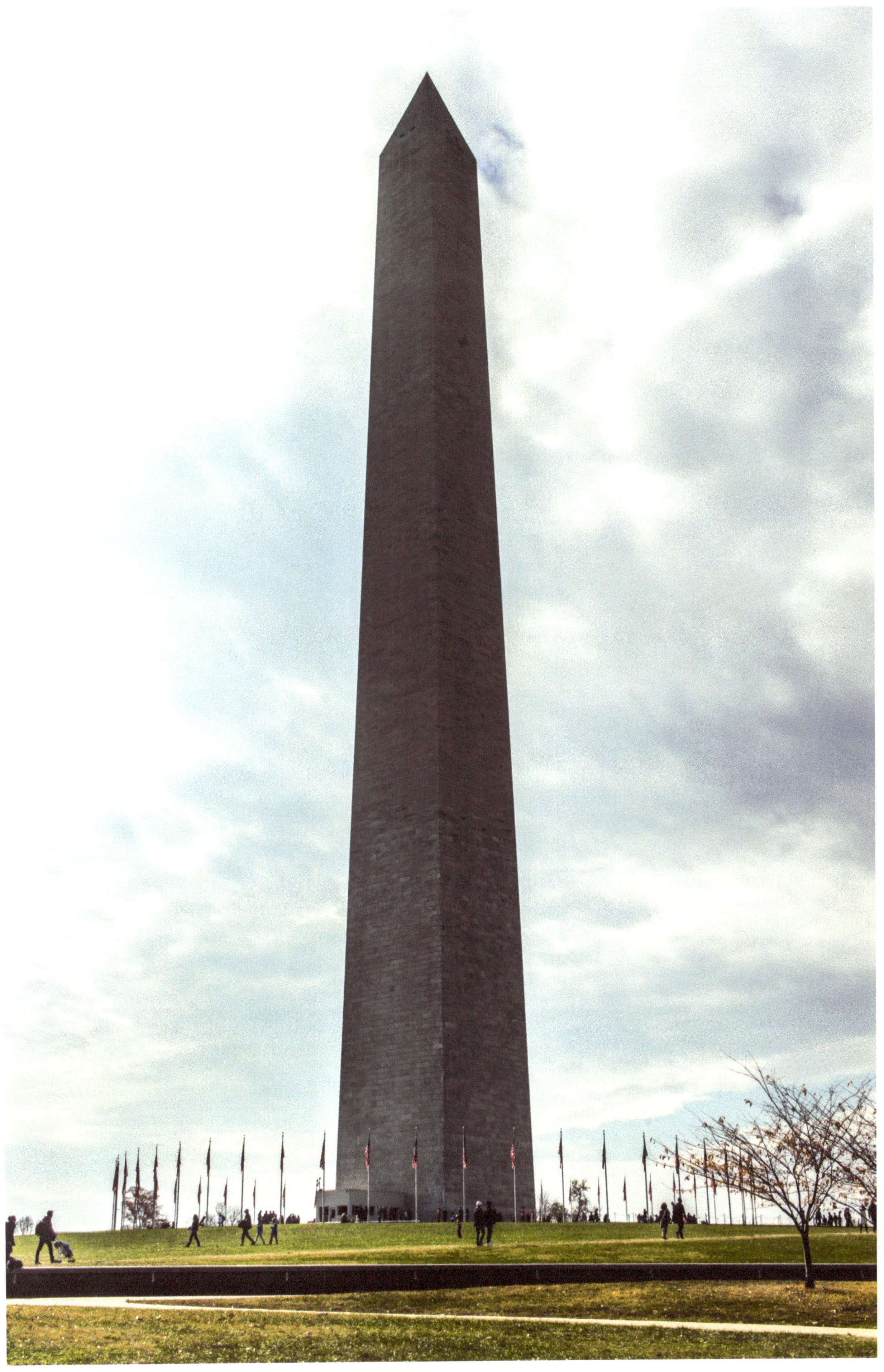

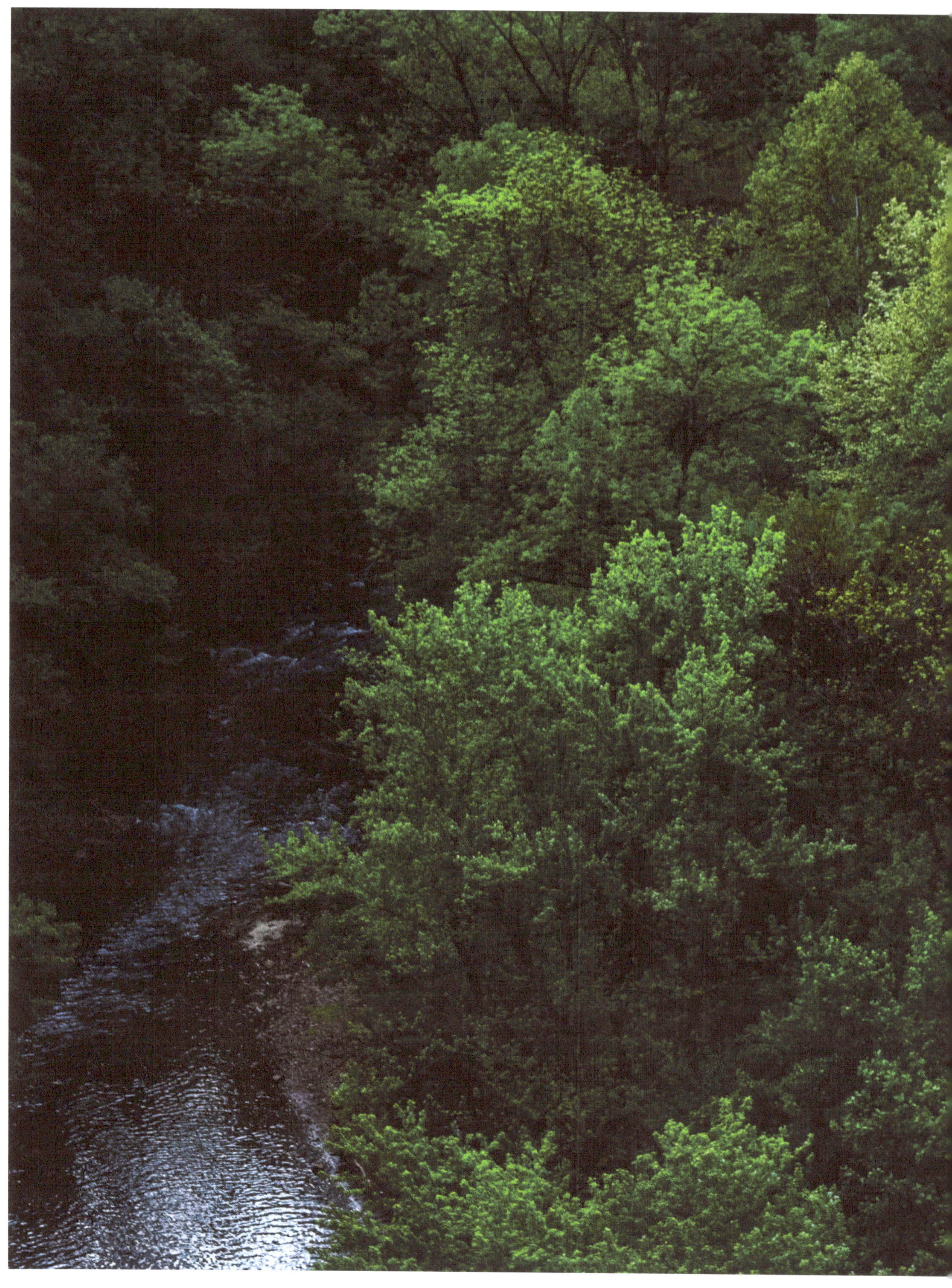

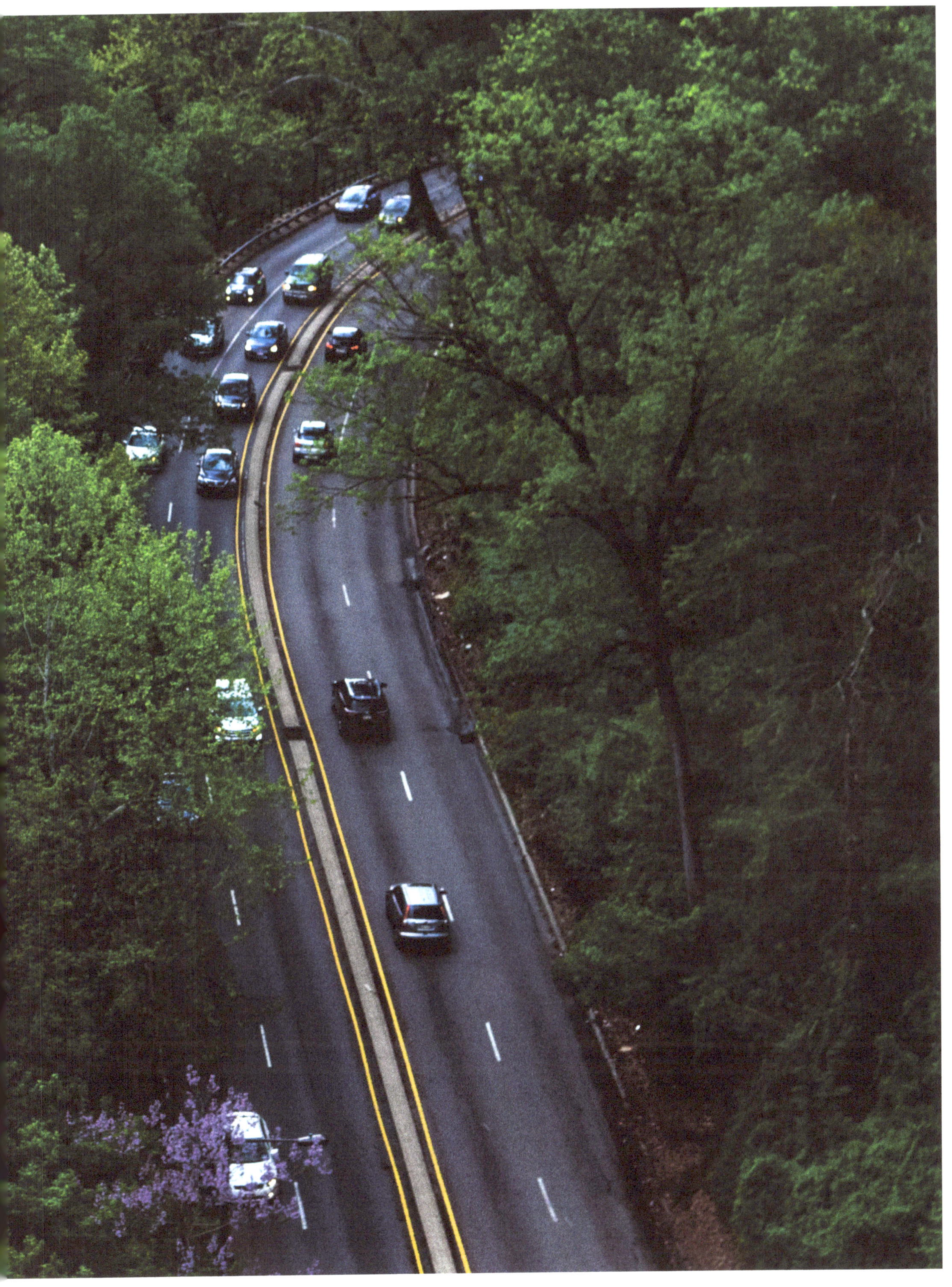

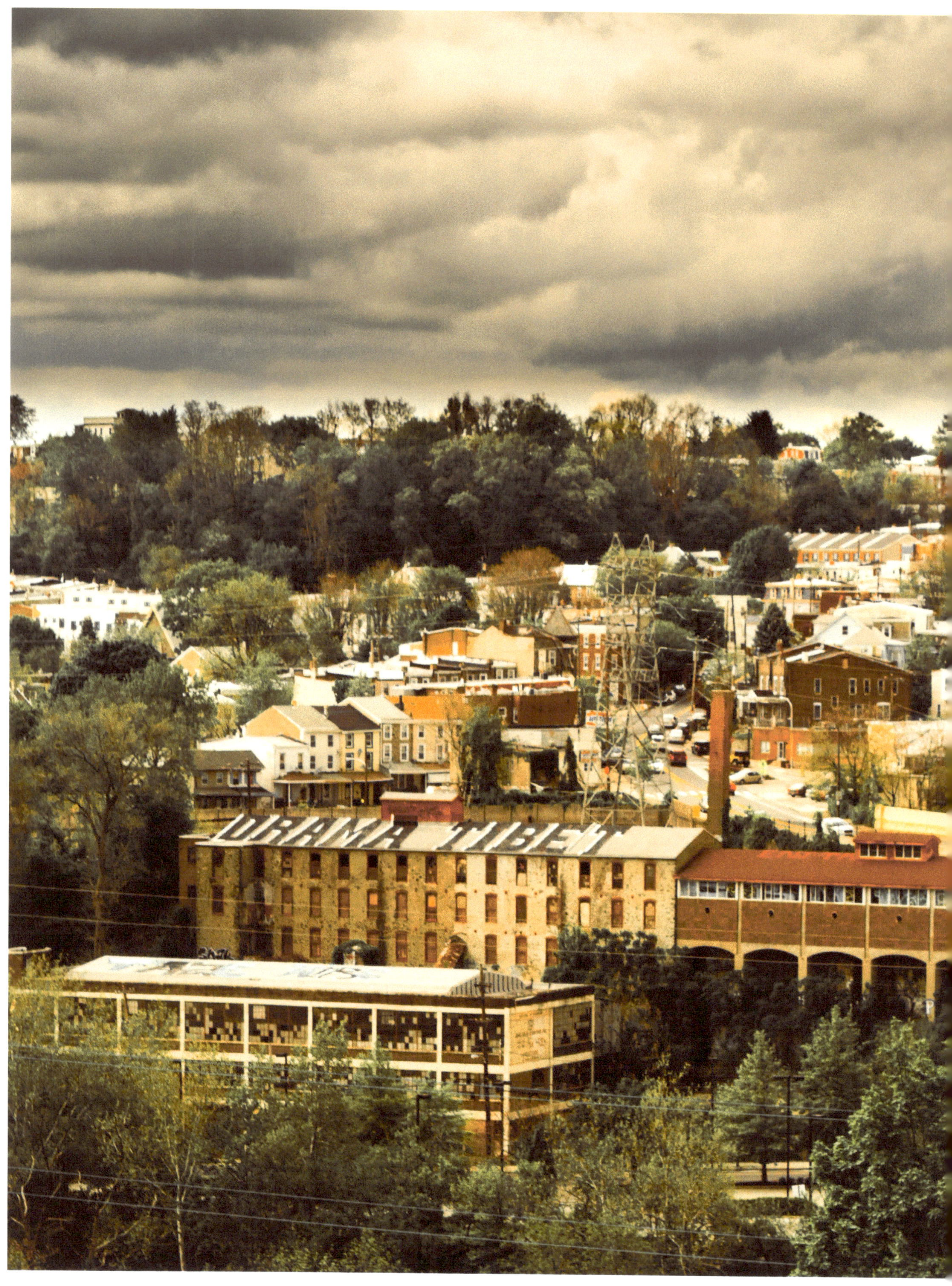
DRAMA TIBET

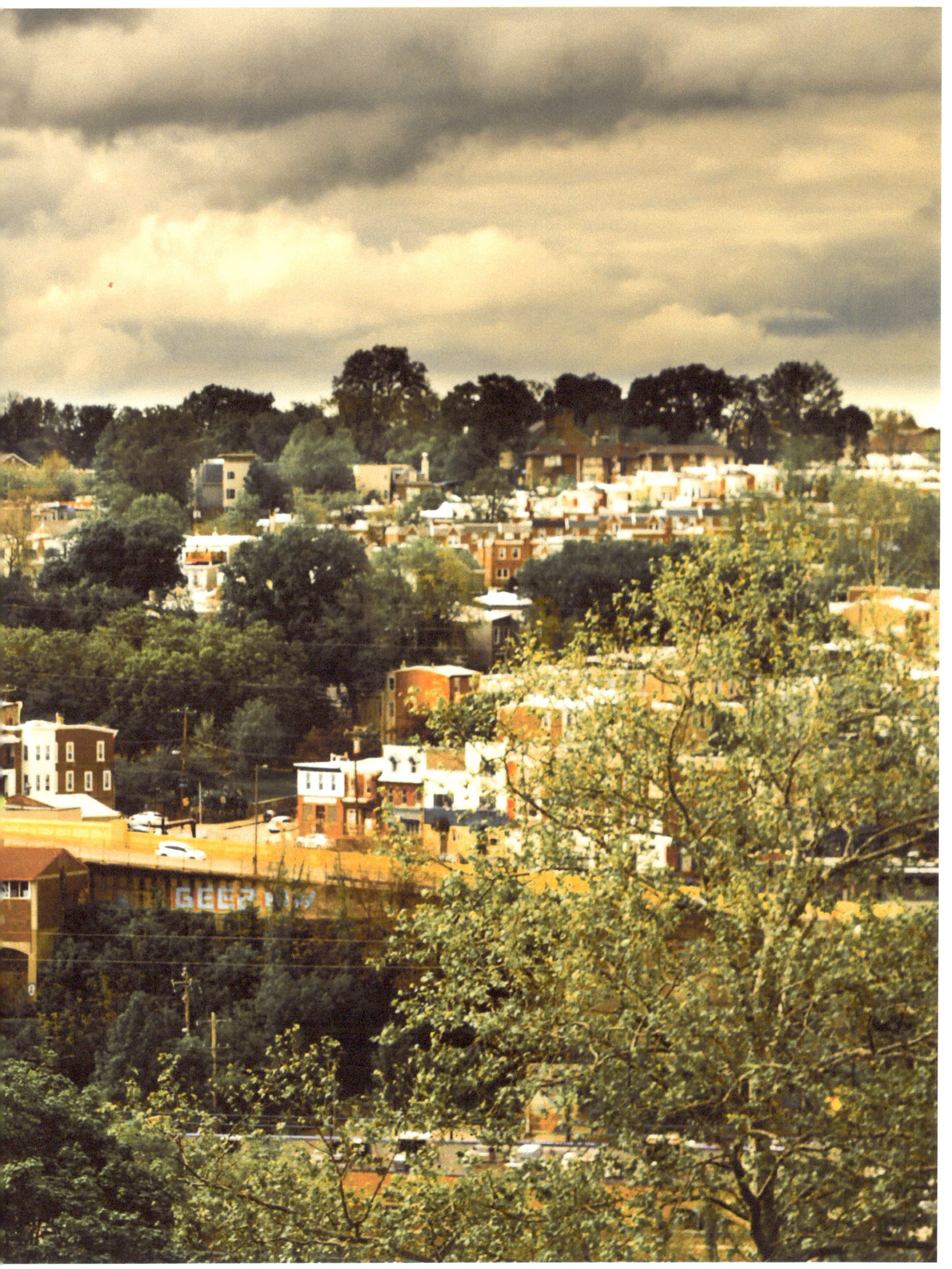

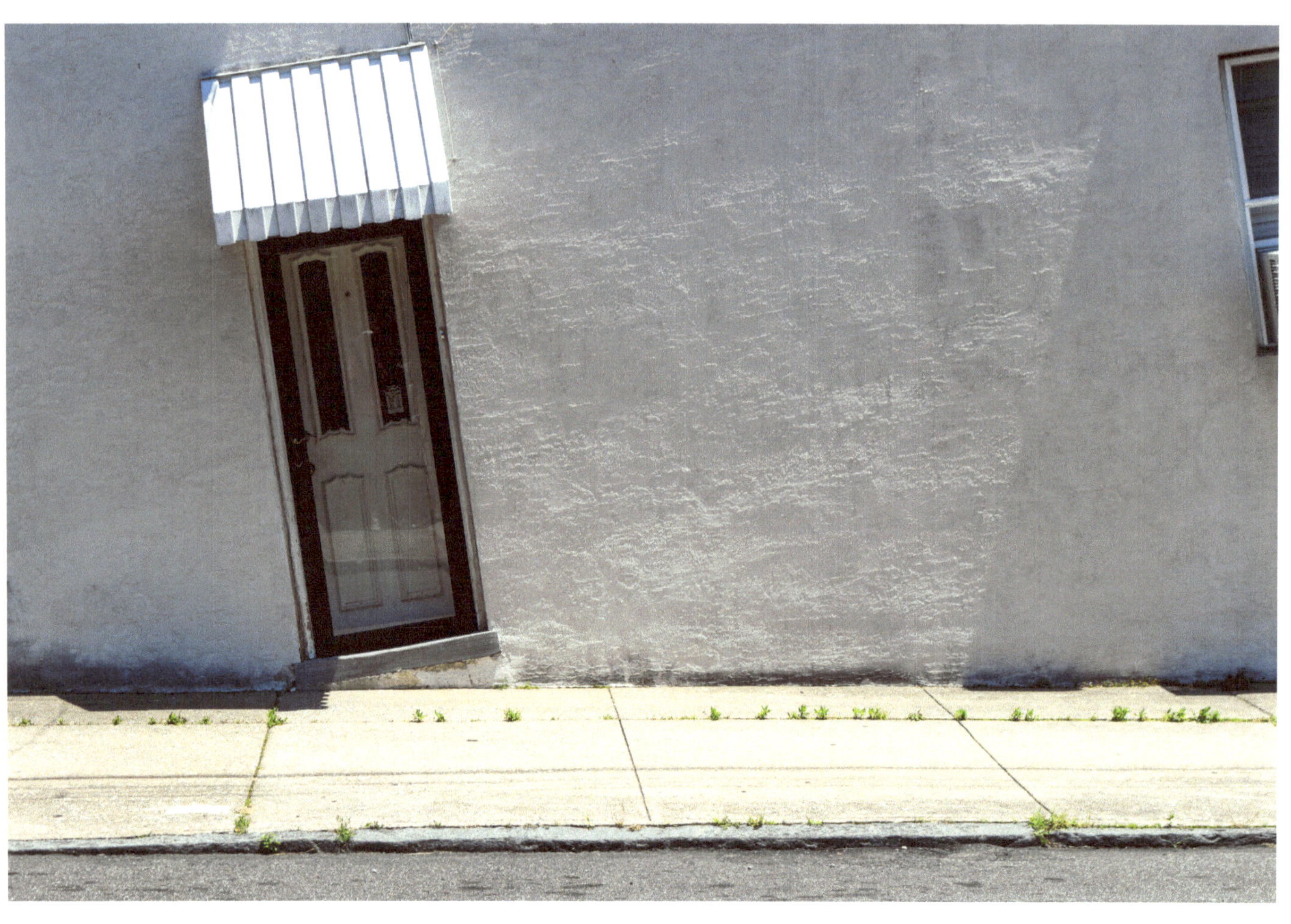

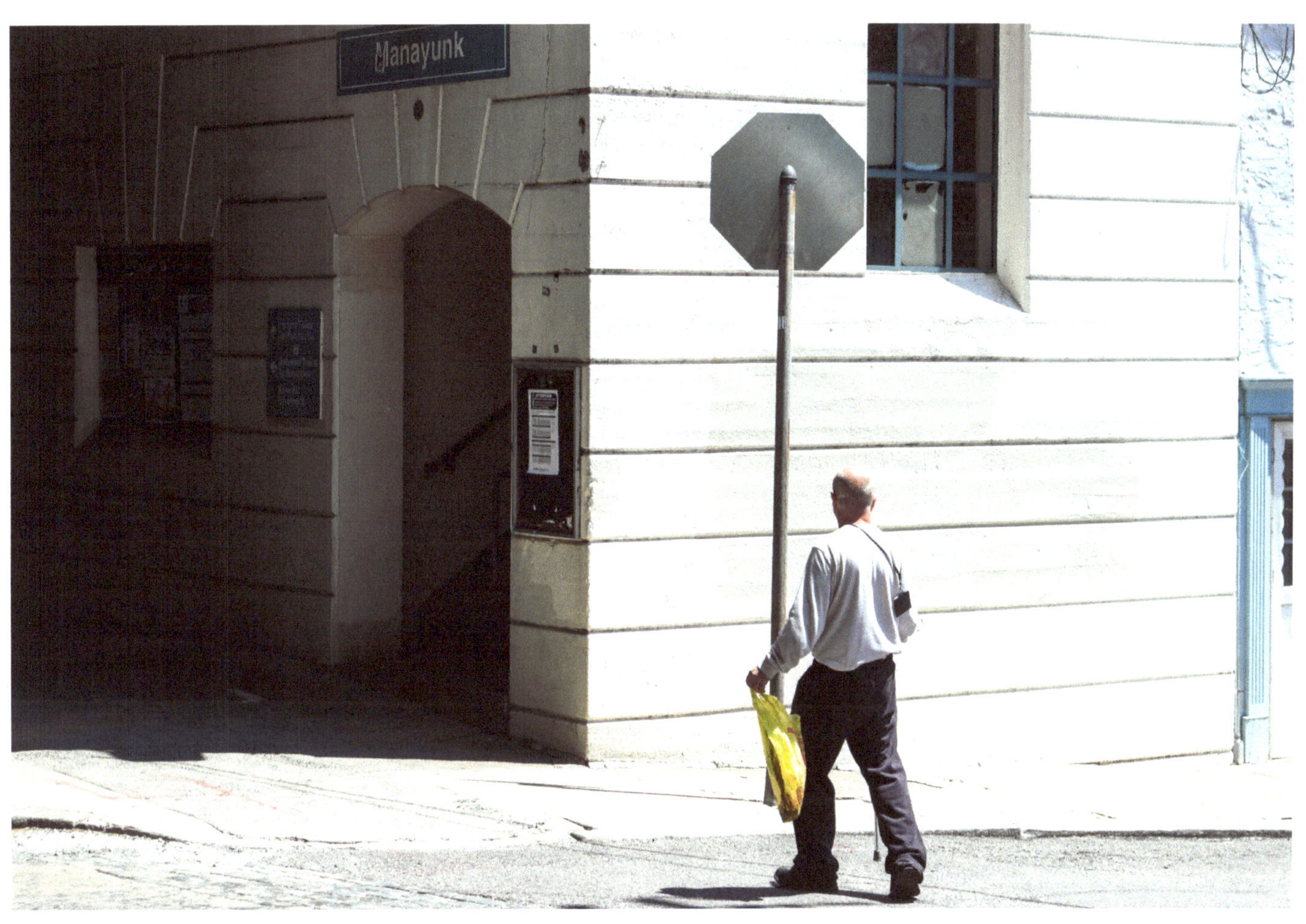
Manayunk

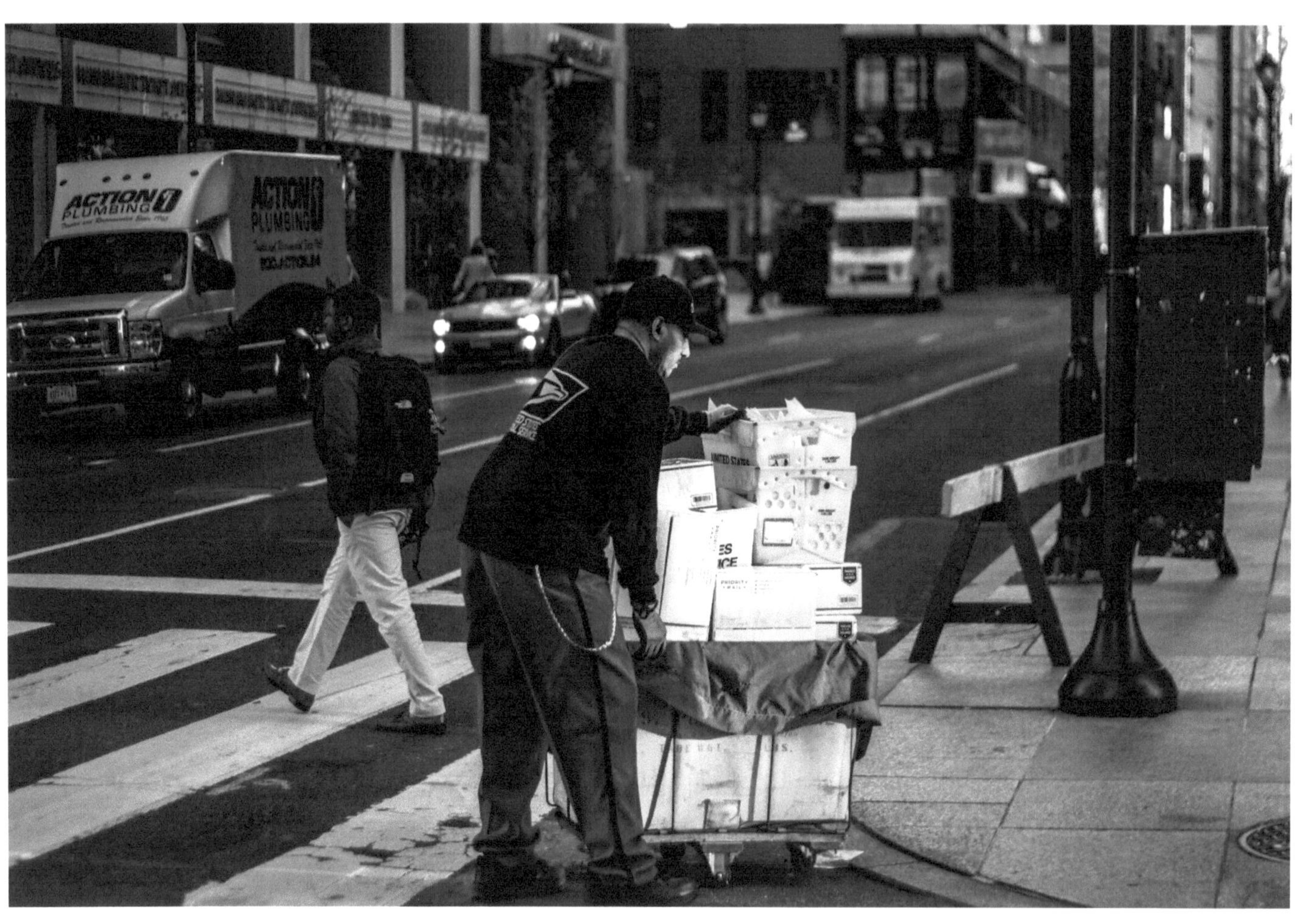
ACTION
PLUMBING
ACTION
PLUMBING

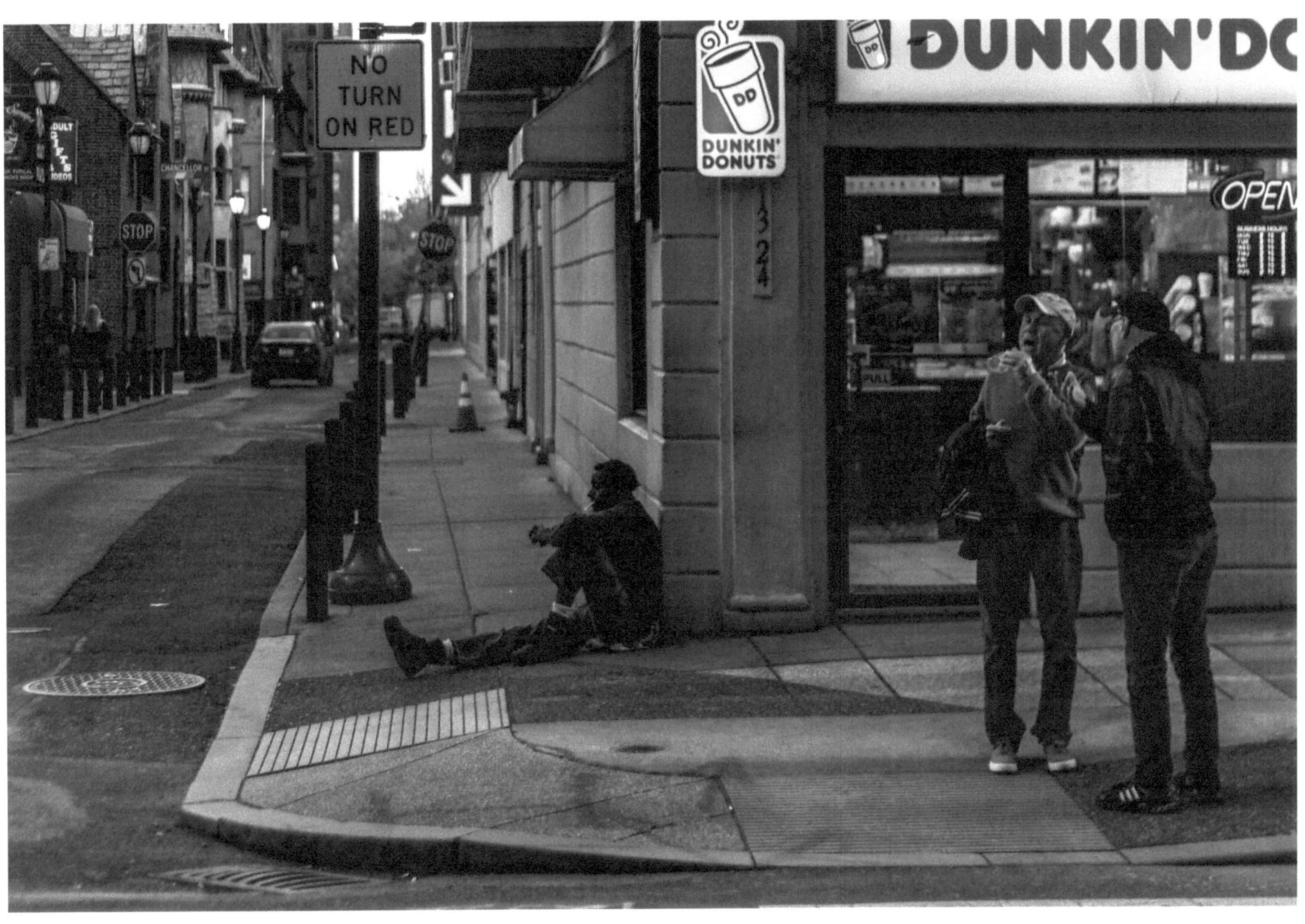
NO
TURN
ON RED
DUNKIN' DONUTS
STOP
1324
OPEN

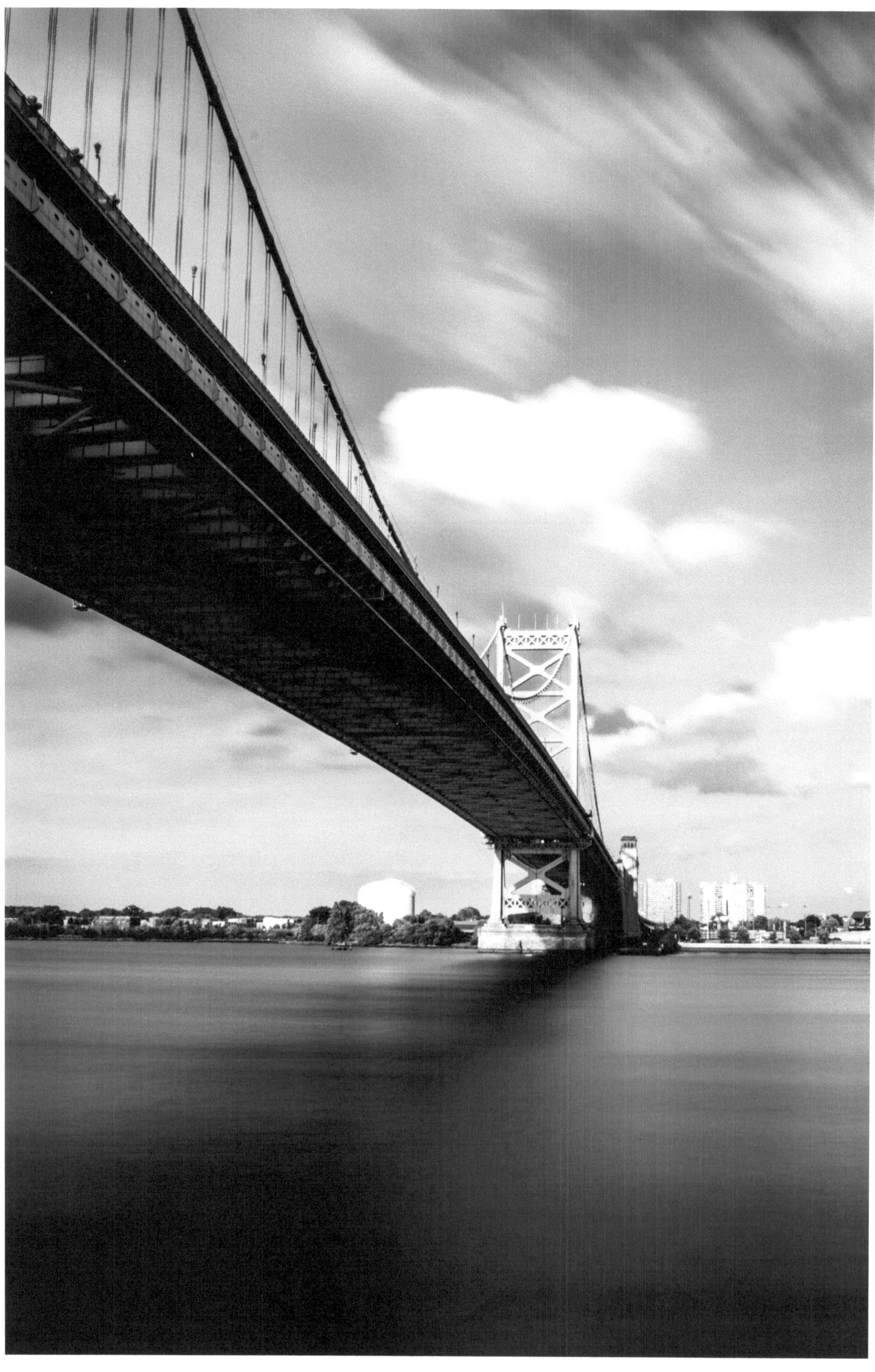

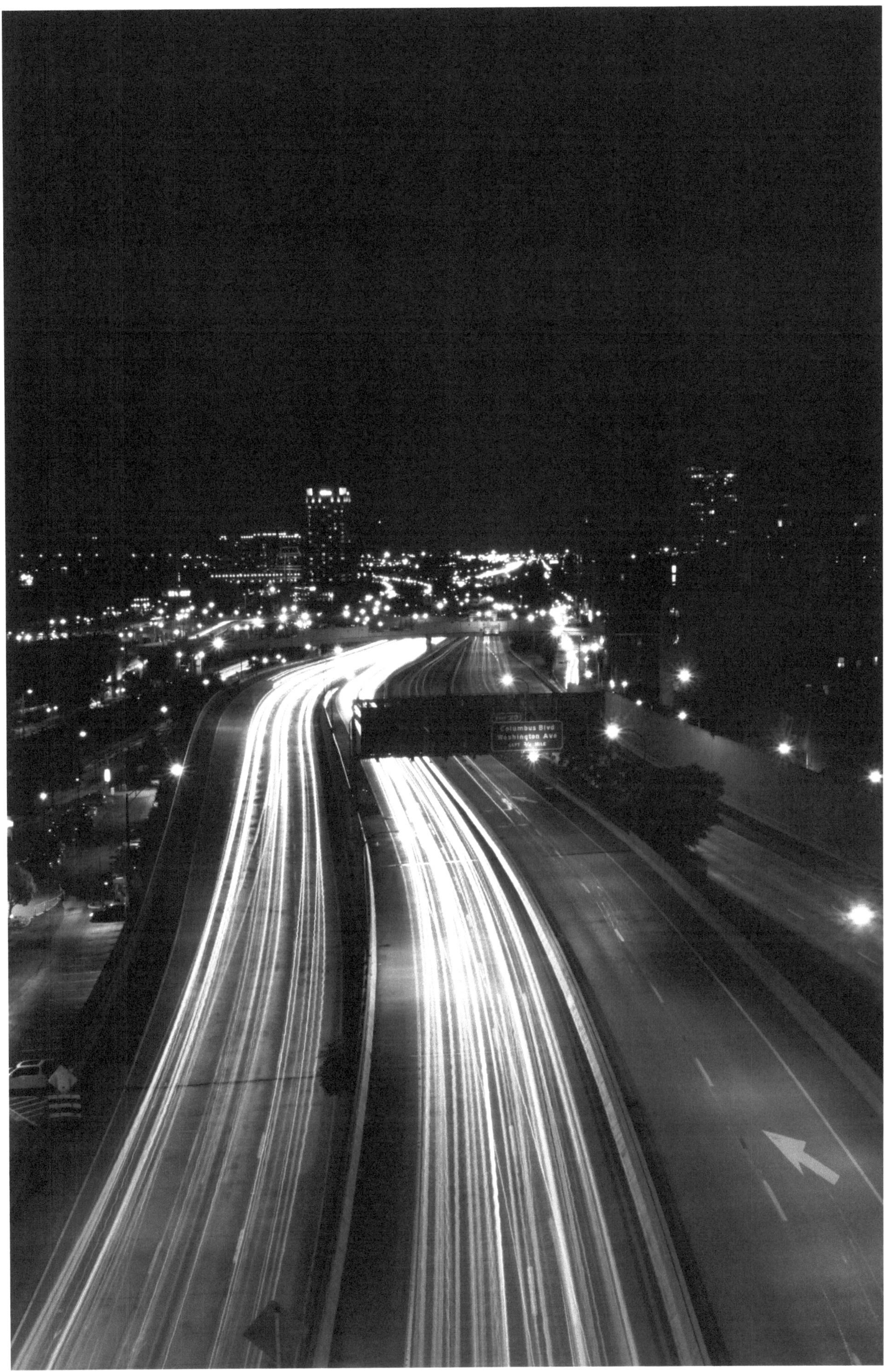
Columbus Blvd
Washington Ave

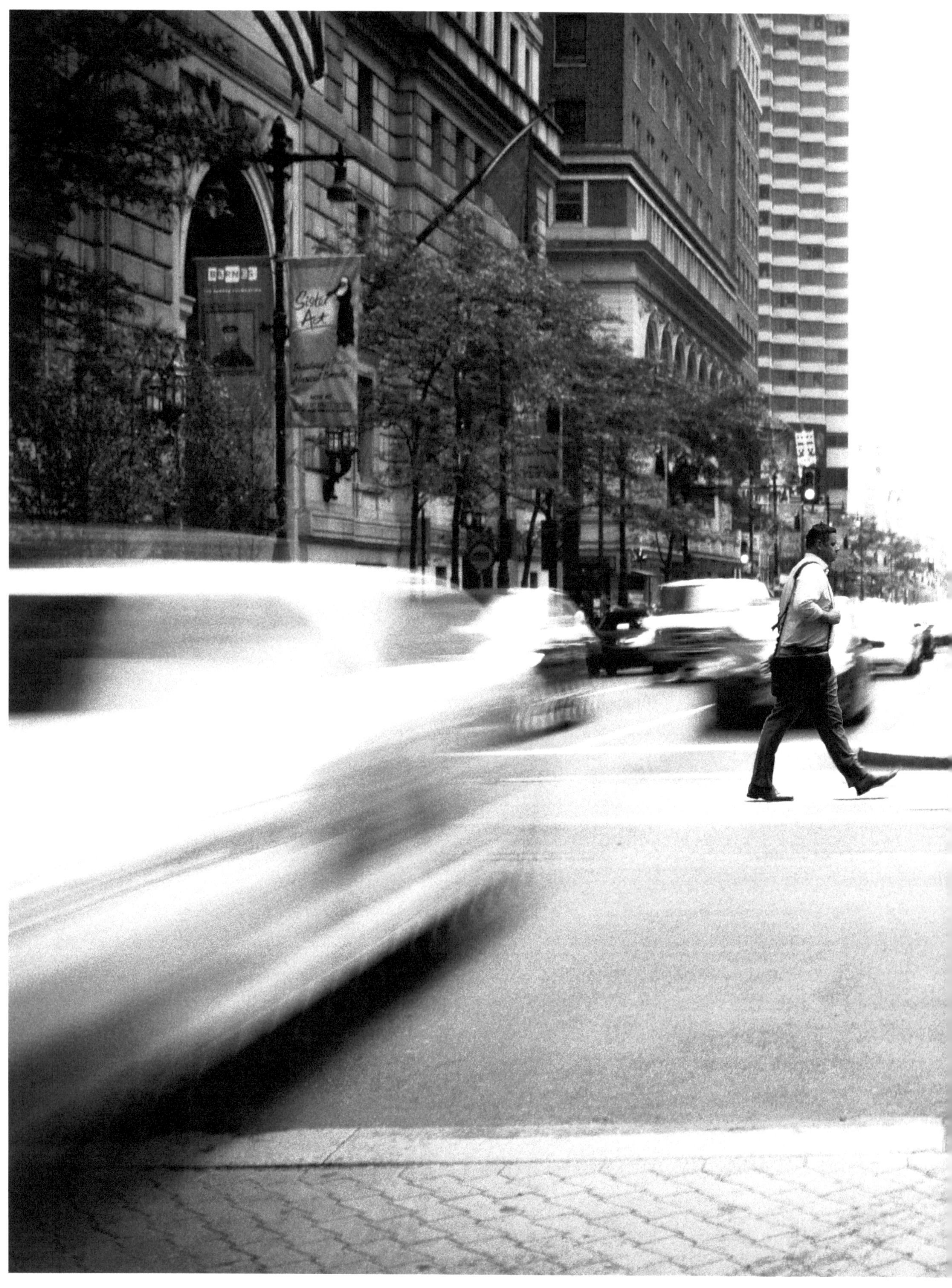
Sister Act

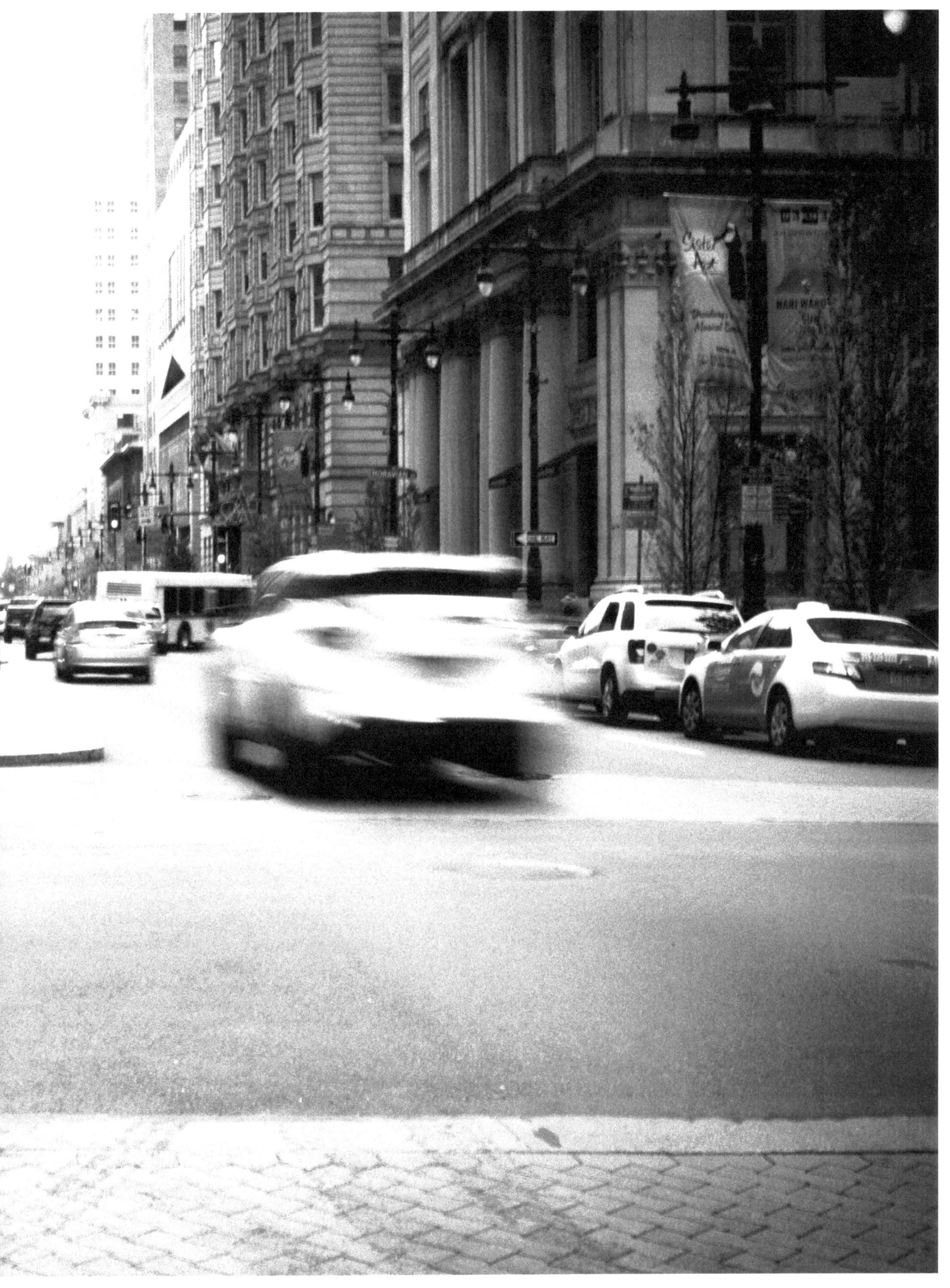

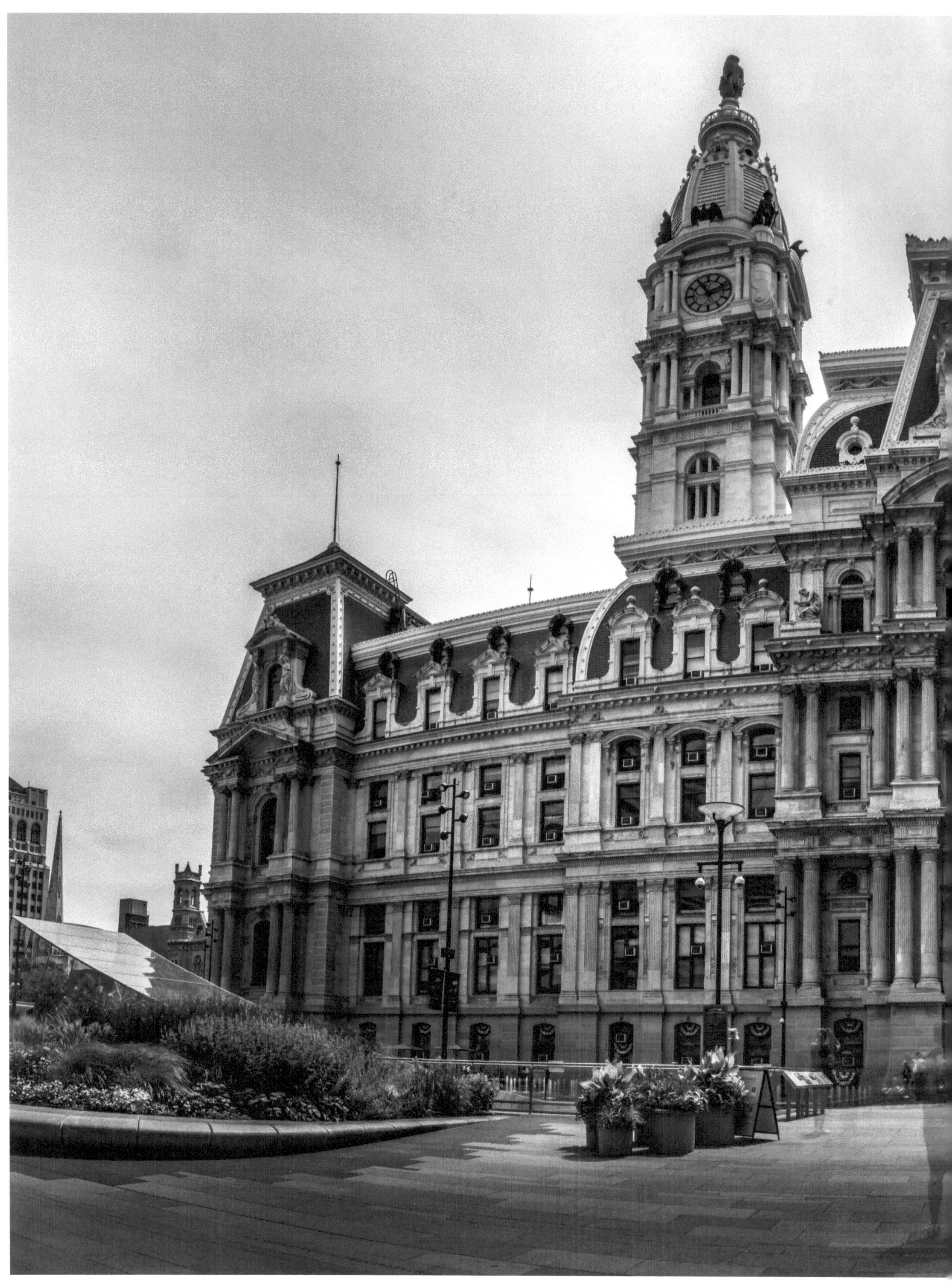

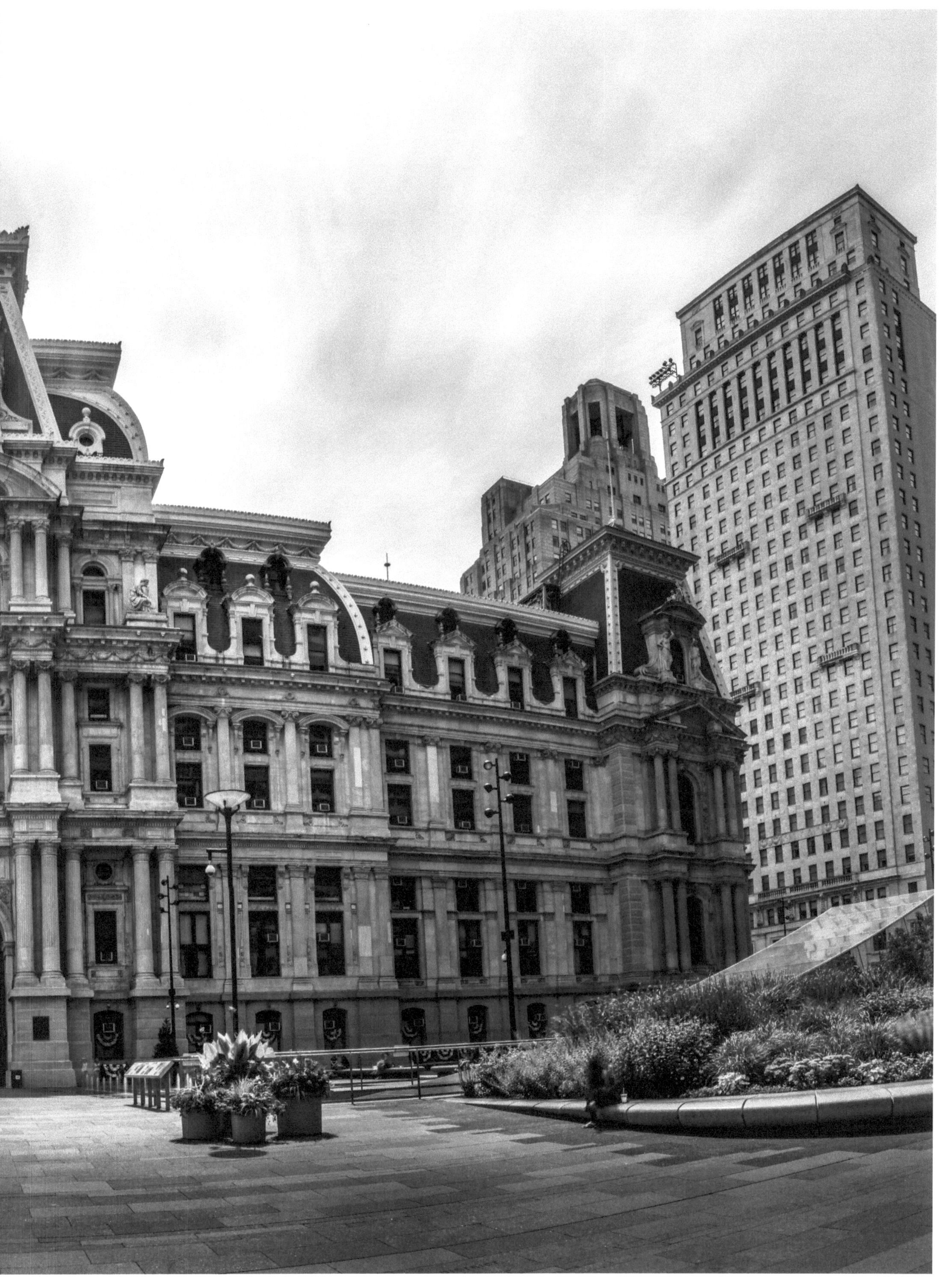

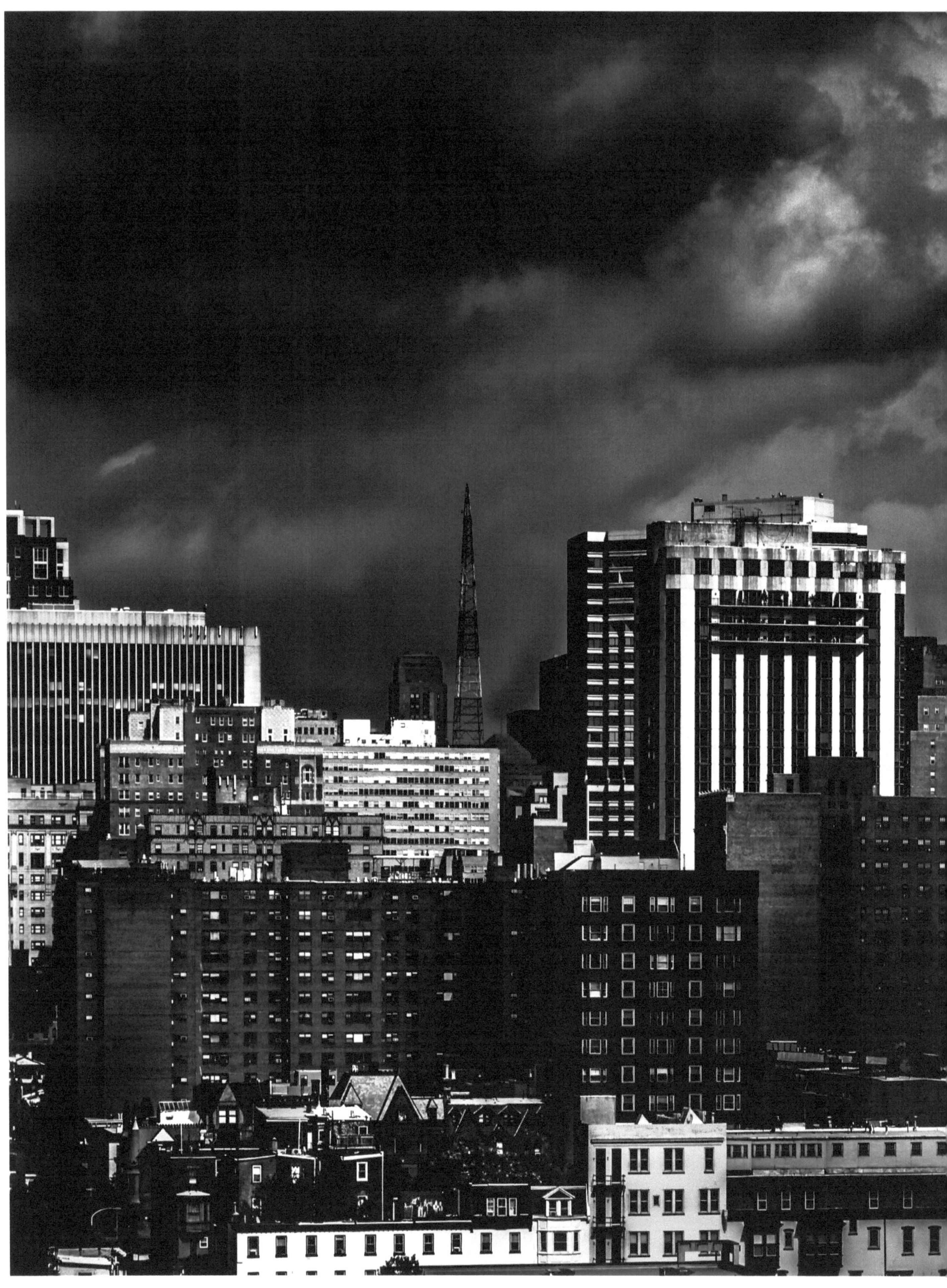

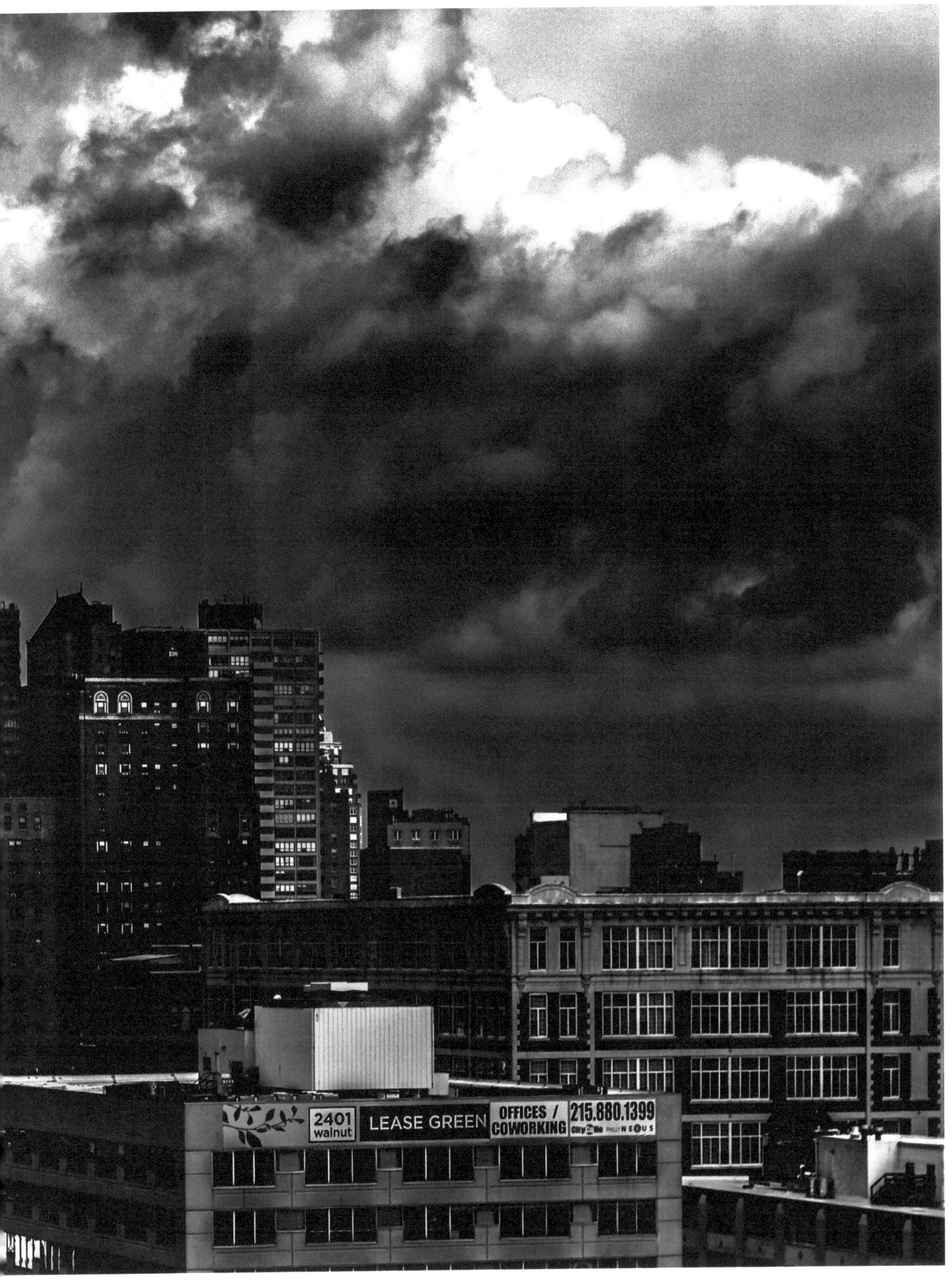
2401 walnut
LEASE GREEN
OFFICES / COWORKING
215.880.1399

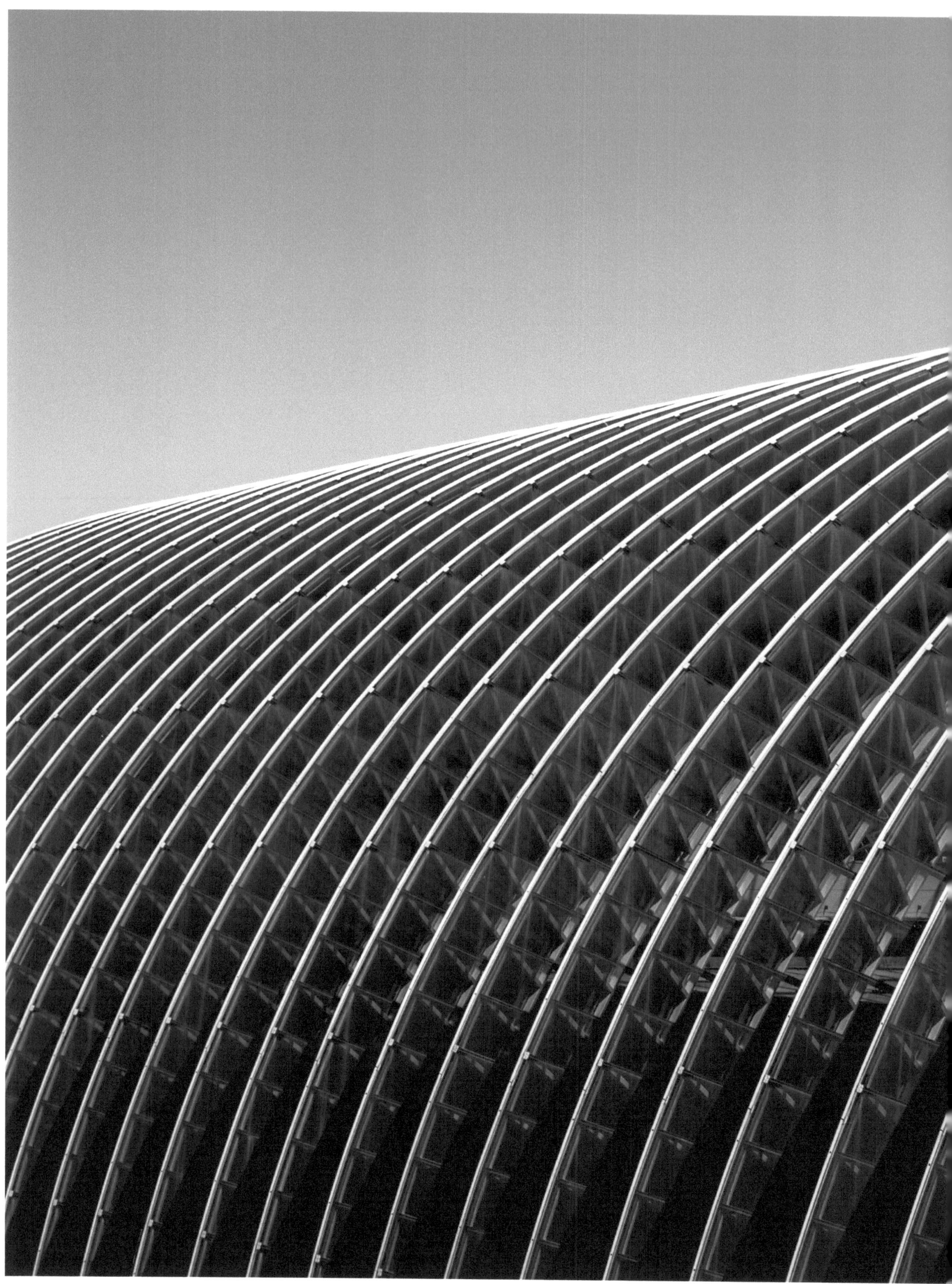

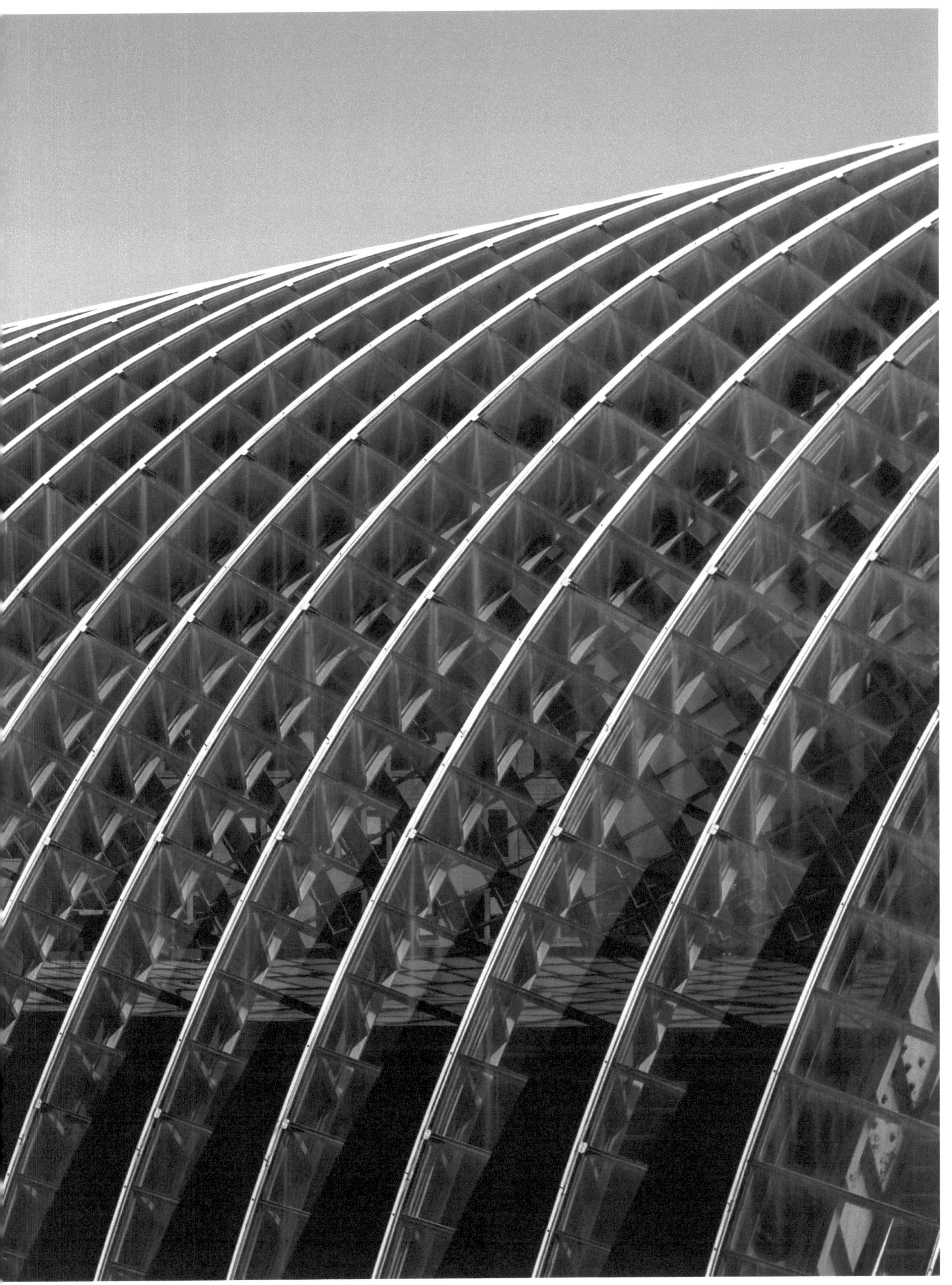

FM1

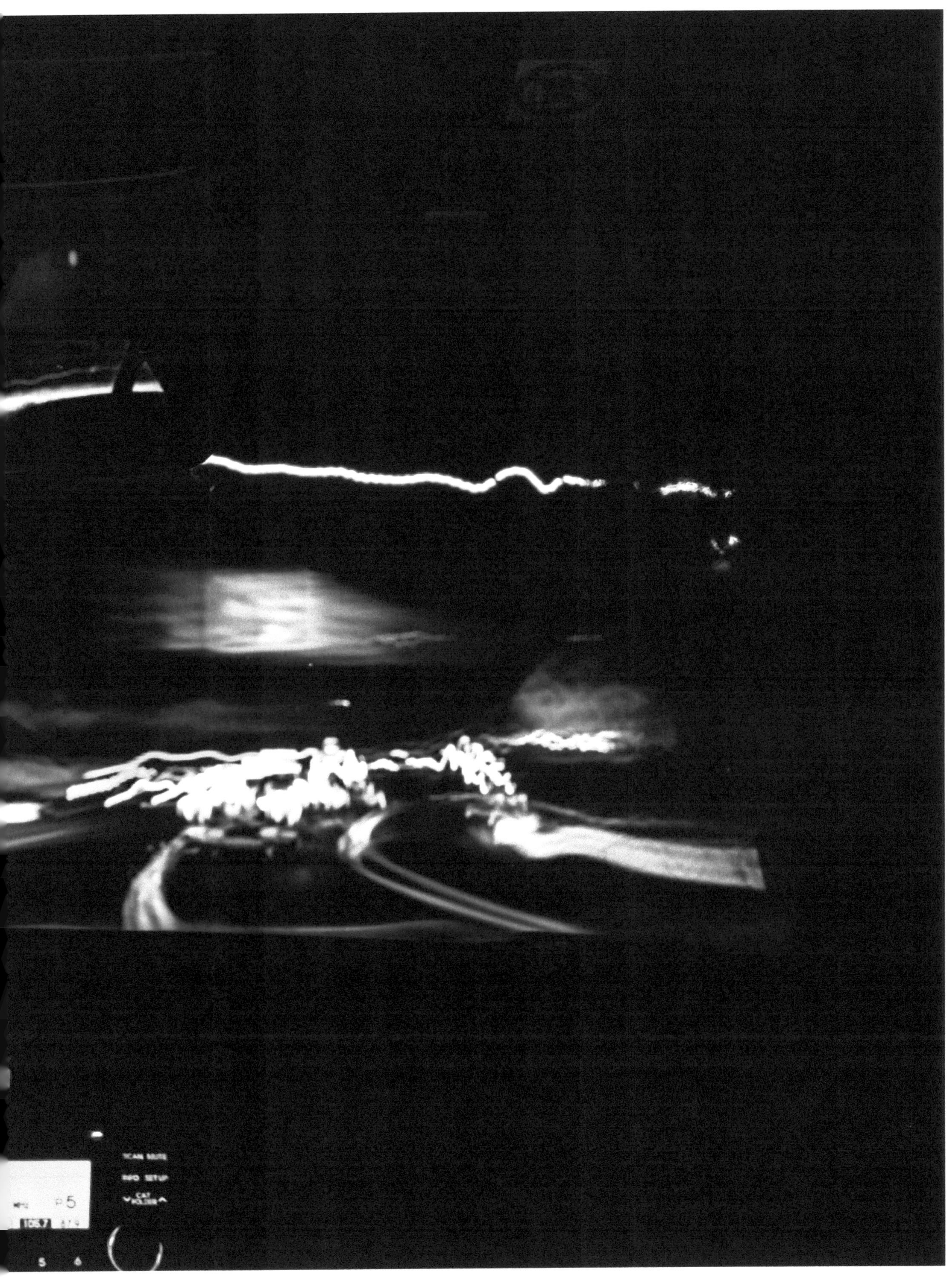
SETUP
CAT
P5

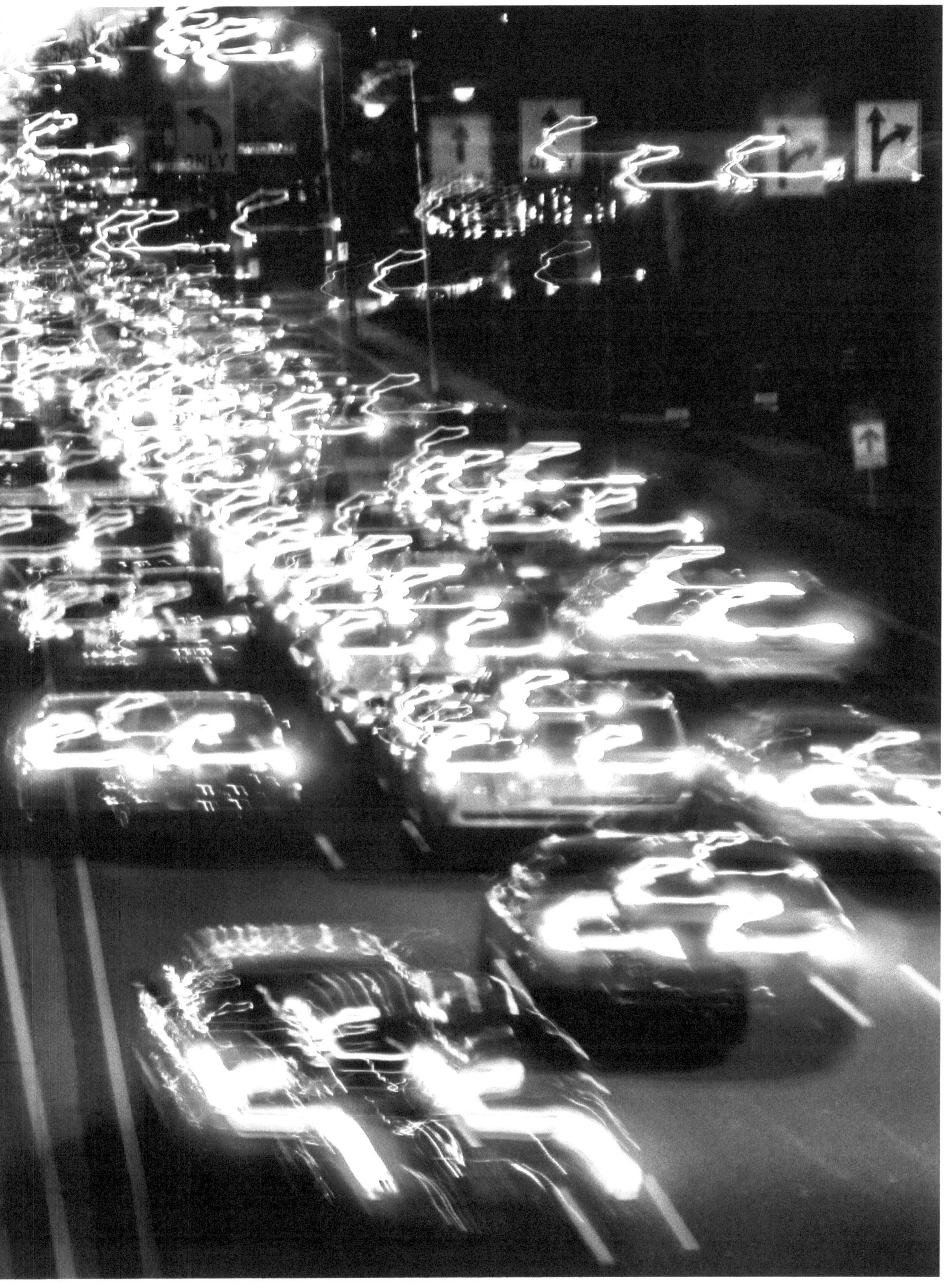
ONLY

INDEX

iii

Architecture

Sculpture

Drawing

Design

Painting

Photography

Photography (cont.)

P. 102 - 103
Lincoln Drive
April, 2016

P. 104 - 105
Manayunk
May, 2016

P. 106
East Falls
June, 2016

P. 107
Old Man Walking
June, 2016

P. 108
USPS
April, 2016

P. 109
Some Eat While Others Starve
April, 2016

P. 110
Benjamin Franklin Bridge
July, 2016

Photography (cont.)

P. 111
Columbus Boulevard
July, 2016

P.112 - 113
Broad Street
June, 2016

P. 114 - 115
City Hall
July, 2016

P. 116 - 117
Center City
June, 2016

P. 118 - 119
Kimmel Center
June, 2016

P.120 - 121
Night Drive
November, 2016

P. 122 - 123
City Avenue
February, 2016

Jonathan Plass
www.jonathanplass.com

www.ingramcontent.com/pod-product-compliance
Ingram Content Group UK Ltd.
Pitfield, Milton Keynes, MK11 3LW, UK
UKHW060106300726
14090UKWH00003B/389

* 9 7 8 0 6 9 2 8 4 7 7 5 6 *